Mouse Pin Trading

The Complete Guide to the Fun and Obsessive World of Disney Pin Trading!

By: The Edgar and
Shilensky Families

Legal Stuff

This book makes reference to various Disney copyrighted characters, trademarks, marks, and registered marks owned by the Walt Disney Company and Walt Disney Enterprises.

All references to these characters and trademarks are used solely for editorial purposes. Neither the authors nor the publisher makes any commercial claim to their use, and neither is affiliated with the Walt Disney Company or its affiliates.

All characters and theme park graphics, as well as the pins themselves, are copyright © The Walt Disney Company.

Dedication

This book is dedicated to the Disney Cast Members who work every day to make us believe that the world can be a magical place, to the Disney Pin Traders who pass on their knowledge, experience, and love of all things Disney and to our families who share our love, our joy, and YES... our obsession!

Acknowledgments

Mouse Pin Trading would like to acknowledge the generations of Pin Traders who have tirelessly posted, blogged, and tweeted to share their knowledge of Disney Pin Trading. Like almost everyone else out there, once we got the Pin Trading bug, we went hunting for more information.

Sites like OfficialDisneyPins.com, PinPics.com, and Dizpins.com contributed to our education and we would like to thank them for fuelling our Pin Trading Obsession.

We would also like to thank Heidi and Cathy for their support and constructive input.

About This Book

When we were putting this book together, there was one thing about Pin Trading we didn't know... YOU!

We didn't know if you were a seasoned trader looking for more info or a newbie who was just getting set to trade your first pin, so we stuck a pin in the board and decided to give you everything. Just like pin trading, this book is an exploration of what we like to call "Pinformation!"

Pins + Information = Pinformation!

How can we explain that a bit better? You know how when you're walking down Main Street, you notice a few things at once. You notice how Main Street flows and makes sense. If you want to find something specific, it's right where you think it should be. At the same time, you notice how cool details are tucked away in the corners so if you want to meander your way through the alleys and shops, and explore the nooks and crannies, you discover amazing details... well it's the same with this book!

The information included in this book flows so it's easy to find, but at the same time, we tucked juicy bits of "pin-formation" in between the checklists, resources, and detail. So how you use this book is up to you...

You can bolt straight to the Checklists and Glossary for specific pinformation, or pick a page and check out the pins and the Mouse Pin Trading Tips scattered throughout the pages. Oh, by the way, all the pictures used in the book are pictures of actual Disney Trading Pins and there are dozens of Hidden Mickey's throughout the pages. How many can you find?

It's our hope that this guide becomes an essential and fun tool in your Pin Trading Toolbox and that you refer to it often through every step of your Disney Pin Trading journey...

Now, let's get trading!

CONTENTS

The Tale of the Pin

Welcome to the amazing and occasionally obsessive world of Disney Pin Trading!

Pin Trading at Disney Parks is a fun and interactive way to interact with Disney Cast Members and other Disney Guests while discovering cool and sometimes valuable pins along the way. Pin Trading is open to anyone above the age of 3. All it takes is a few pins, a lanyard and a desire to expand your Disney Park experience! Pixie Dust is optional, but always good to have on hand...

This guide is compiled from my family's personal pin trading experience in Disneyland and Walt Disney World. We felt it would be a great idea to share our experience in Pin Trading as we have definitely seen what works and what can cost you a ton of money and frustration. By sharing our experience, we hope that this guide will assist you on your Pin Trading Adventures and help to map out a few exciting points of interest along the way.

You don't have to be a Professional Pin Trader to have a great Disney Pin Trading experience. In fact, the whole program is designed for all Disney guests, from the folks on their first Visit, to the Annual Pass Holders who are in the park every week to be able to interact and talk about their favorite Disney Characters. We have met some amazing people through pin trading and it's a fantastic way to meet people from all over the world with a commonality – they all love Disney!

Mouse Pin Trading Tip!

Most Cast Members are also Pin Traders, so they have a wealth of knowledge. When you have some downtime in your day, ask them what they collect. You never know where the conversation may lead. There is a Cast Member who works in Custodial (the folks who keep everything bright and shiny) in Downtown Disney named Tom. The first time we met him, we traded pins and then chatted for a few minutes. The next day, he had several pins that my kids had been looking for, and the next day, and the day after that. Tom still works there and every time we see him, he pulls out his bag of pins.

Ready for the amazing part? To this day, he remembers all of our favorite Disney Characters!

My family first got interested in Disney pins during our very first visit to Disneyland when my son and daughter were 7 and 9. We have been back to a Disney Park at least twice a year since that first visit and pin trading has become a main ingredient for a memorable trip. When it comes to Disney Pin Trading we need to make sure we maximize our time in the park because it's not like we will be back next week to complete a pin set (we actually live in Vancouver, BC). We found that most of the pin traders we were meeting were Local Resident Pass Holders who were in the park at least twice a month, so most of their advice was not of any use to us.

It's great that if you live in Southern California or Orlando you can pop into the park whenever a cool pin is being released, but for us regular vacation types, what can we do?

Well, using the information we are going to share with you in this guide, my family has been able to trade an average of 300 – 400 pins in a 5 day visit to the park... and go on all our favorite attractions... and get 40 or more Disney Character Signatures, all with just a little planning and insight.

Like I said, we know how to maximize our time at Disney!

When you really dive into Disney Pin Trading, there can be a lot of information to digest, so we will do our best to simplify as much as possible and make sure you have the Pin Trading lingo you need to enjoy your experience without becoming overwhelmed.

So, in the words of that eternal Lost Boy, Peter Pan... "HERE WE Gooooooo!"

Fun Park Words Series

Lollipop Mystery Series

How Did We Get Started?

Confessions of a Disney Pin Addict

The first time we took the family to Disneyland, we knew we were going to "Go Big", so we budgeted for everything... or so we thought. We budgeted for the Character Breakfast and Dinners, lots of Souvenirs, a "Discover the Magic Tour"... we even had a Turkey Leg and Pickle budget! What we didn't account for were all these really cool lanyards covered with bright shiny Disney pins that every one was wearing... and they were trading other bright shiny pins with Disney Cast Members!

We had to get in on the action!

So we ran to the nearest store (fortunately there is a shopping opportunity every 20 feet or so in a Disney Park and asked how to get started. A very helpful Cast Member (who was wearing a lanyard full of princess pins that my daughter wanted to trade for) walked us over to the Pin Section and we were on our way.

Our first Pin Trading bill read like this:

Tinkerbell Starter Set with Lanyard:	$44.95
Sorcerer Mickey Starter Set:	$44.95
Regular Adult Lanyard:	$8.95
Tinkerbell Lanyard Medallion:	$9.95
Sorcerer Mickey Lanyard Medallion:	$9.95
4 Pin Starter Set	$22.95
Total (not including taxes)	$141.70

That sound you hear is our budget flying away to Neverland... but we're good to go, right? Not so much. You see we were foolish enough to spend a lot of time pointing out all the really cool pins and pin sets, so when it came to trading, neither of our children wanted to trade their pins! They didn't even want to trade the duplicates on the lanyard set!

So... back to the pin rack to pick out the ugliest pins we could find. Add to the tab:

4 Pin Starter Set #2:	$22.95
4 Pin Starter Set #3:	$22.95
	$44.90

That puts the running total at: $187.60

Now we're all set! We have pins, our lanyards are bright and shiny and we are surrounded by smiling Cast Members who let us know that we can each trade up to 2 pins with them per day. Perfect!

Our inventory of trading pins lasted exactly 16 minutes.

Fortunately, we hadn't even managed to make our way out of the store yet, so the pin rack was close by! I franticly started looking through each box of starter pins looking for the best deal (now thinking on a cost per pin basis) and found out that the magic of Disney also extended to their pricing strategy!

Every pin set worked out to $4.27 per pin or more, when we looked at packs with 7 pins in the set (4 pin sets worked out to an even higher price per pin). Let's face it, the people behind the Mouse know how to create an experience and they also know how to make a buck!

To make a long cash register receipt short, by the end of our first day in Disneyland, we had purchased and traded a total of 72 pins. The price tag for our new addiction (including lanyards and a few Limited Edition Pins) was $544.00 (not including tax, of course) and the stack of receipts looked like "Walt's Life Story". That, combined with the "what happened to the budget?" look on my wife's face should have been the last chapter of our Disney Pin story, but we were hooked.

We spread our lanyards and the pins that would not fit on the lanyards out on the bed and basked in their shiny brilliance. We spent the next hour examining our booty and sorting each pin by character. My son was collecting Sorcerer Mickey and Stitch Pins, My daughter was collecting Tinkerbell and Princess Pins and my wife (despite the disapproving look on her face) had managed to gather a sizeable Eeyore collection. As I was mainly responsible for inventory (running back and forth between the store and my family) and didn't have a lanyard of my own, but there were still a good number of Grumpy Pins that were collected on my behalf!

All was going well... and then my daughter noticed a small Mickey Head on one of her Tink pins... and then another... and another! I picked one up, turned it over and read those words that forever changed our Pin Trading world – "Cast Lanyard Collection" – "Pin 2 of 10"

There were collections hidden amongst our new found pins! We knew we had no choice but to complete the collections... and that would require more traders.

Fortunately for us, The World of Disney Store was open until midnight and within walking distance of the hotel, so we could stock up before we got to the park in the morning and not waste a moment of trading time!

By the end of our first Disney vacation, we had spent over $1,200.00 in pins, completed the entire Cast Lanyard Series for that year, plus more than half of the previous year's collection and our suitcases were heavier by about 6 pounds.

We travelled back to Vancouver, already discussing what type of pins would be out at Christmas and planning our next trip to The Happiest Place on Earth... and then I looked at the expression on my wife's face. I knew from that expression that if I wanted to keep up my newly found obsession, I needed to find a way to make it more cost effective. Adding $1200.00 to the Disney budget for trading pins wasn't going to fly no matter how much Pixie Dust I threw at it, and our new obsession with Disney Pins could actually squash our chances of ever coming back, if we didn't find an option.

Mouse Pin Trading Tip!

Note to Moms: She was right of course...

Spending thousands of dollars on pins was out of the question, and if you plan on Pin Trading as part of your Disney Trip you need to have a budget. Let me rephrase that: Your family is going to want to trade pins and even if your children are too young to trade themselves, then you are going to want to collect for them! Pin Trading is part of the Disney experience and an amazing way to meet people. Again, if your experience is anything like ours, they are going to want to trade pins, so have the discussion and plan for it, so you don't have a "Non-magical Moment" in the middle of Main Street!

Don't get me wrong, we had an absolute blast trading almost 200 pins, met some great people and had some amazing conversations, but reality kicks in when you have to pay the Visa bill, so it was time to correct and continue - Christmas was only 10 months away!

We started our Disney Pin Education by finding out just how many types of Disney Pins there were to trade, and to be traded and there are a ton! We found that the more familiar we were with what was out there, the better we were at making trades and talking to other pin traders. Here's what we found...

It All Started with a Mouse... Pin.

Collectible pins have always been part of the Disney experience, but Pin Trading officially started in Walt Disney World in 1999 during the Millennium Celebration, spreading to Disneyland California the following year. Since then, over 90,000 pins have been released by Disney in various editions and collections. Pins that were released exclusively in one park will say on the back which Disney Park it came from, including Paris, Tokyo and Hong Kong. To help you sort through the smorgasbord of Disney pins, here is a breakdown of the types of pins that Disney produces.

- ♥ **Cast Lanyard or Hidden Mickey Pins** have a small Mickey Mouse silhouette hidden somewhere on the face of the pin. These are the pins that moved my family from hobby to obsession. These pins can only be traded for as they are not available for purchase. The pins are released in waves and there will be different collections in each park, so it may be difficult to collect an entire series during one visit. At the start of their shift, hundreds of Disney Cast Members load up their pin lanyards and venture out in the park to do their jobs and extend the pin trading experience with Disney Guests, and these coveted pins are tucked away on those lanyards. Some of these pins are exclusive to one park, while others are part of the **Global Lanyard Series** and will be released across all Disney parks.

 Mᴏᴜsᴇ Pɪɴ Tʀᴀᴅɪɴɢ Tɪᴘ!

Mystery Packs: At random times you can purchase Mystery Paks fo Hidden Mickey pins in the parks. Talk nice to the Cast Member behind the counter and they may even let you feel the package to see if your fingers can find the pin you're looking for. Completer pins are offered the same way.

❤ **Completer Pins** are Disney's way to keep you guessing! Just when you think you've completed a series, you find out there is one more pin. Disney creates a special pin that "Completes" a Cast Lanyard, Special Edition and Gift with Purchase pin series. The Cast Lanyard Completers are found on the Cast Member Lanyards like the regular CL pins, and the GWP pins are randomly placed within the purchase selection. The Special Edition Completer Pins are usually available only at special events. These pins will have "Completer Pin" stamped on the pin back. Some pin sets will have more than one completer and there may be a different completer pin for each park.

- **Gift with Purchase Pins (GWP)** can be purchased at specific Pin Stores in all parks for between $1.00 and $2.95 depending on the collection with a minimum purchase (usually around $30.00). These pins are also given out randomly, so you often see them on Cast Member Lanyards. The last time we were in WDW, we collected the entire postcard set on the first day we were in the park. GWP pins will be stamped "Gift With Purchase" on the back and usually be a numbered (1 of..., 2 of...) set. The first Sunday of each month is designated GWP Day and when these series are released.

- **Rack or Open Edition Pins** are found on the racks in Disney retail shops. They range in price from $6.95 to $15.95 and the selection includes everything from your favorite Disney Character to your favorite Disney Attraction. My family will make a game of trading for rack pins by picking a few we like in the stores and then trying to find them on a lanyard. We do the same thing for pin sets, which are also considered Open Edition. It's amazing what you can find when you pay attention and can trade a pin you don't like for one that retails for $6.95 or more.

 ## Mouse Pin Trading Tip!

As Disney releases new pins every day, keeping track of what pins are available and finding out how, where and when they will be released can get complicated! This book comes with access to our Mouse Pin Trading "PINsider" newsletter, with updates on what's upcoming and what's really, really cool. Register for the "PINsider" newsletter by going to MousePinTrading.com, NOW!

❤ **Limited Edition and Limited Release Pins** are just what they sound like. They are pins with a limited edition size of anywhere between 50 and 5000 and can be a single pin or a pin set. The lower the number, the harder they are to find and the more valuable they are. Throughout the year, Disney will run Limited Release Events where guests are given the opportunity to purchase low edition pins based on a random selection process. Check the Disney Pin Trading site for details and events. Limited Editions will have the words LIMITED EDITION on the back stamp and also note the Edition Size.

- **Cast Member Exclusive Pins** are not to be confused with Cast Lanyard Pins. Cast Member exclusive pins can only be purchased by Cast Members, so they are rare to find in the parks. On top of this, there are also pins that are exclusive to different groups within Disney (IE: Disney Studio's and WDI, Imagineering) so keep an eye out for these extremely exclusive pins. These pins can be Open or Limited Edition and will often commemorate a special event (IE: Earth Day) Imagineering Pins have a Mickey Sorcerer Hat imprinted on the back.

♥ **Artist Proof Pins** will have a small "AP" on the back stamp. Note that AP can also stand for "Annual Passholder". Artist Proof Pins are very rare as they are the actual pins that were used by the artist in the development of the pin. Many of them never made it to mass production, but become available on the secondary market and at special pin trading events.

Mouse Pin Trading Tip!

Annual Passholder Pins can only be purchased if you are a current Annual Pass Holder. This kind of stinks if you only visit the park once or twice a year and can't justify the cost of an annual pass. So what can you do? Talk to people! We have never failed to find someone who offers to use their annual pass to buy us a pin (we pay for it of course) as they are allowed to get 2 pins per pass. You might not feel comfortable asking, but if the opportunity comes up, take it.

♥ Special and Exclusive Pins

Disney loves to commemorate events and acknowledge achievement with pins, so there are a wide variety of pins that can only be found from certain Cast Members and even then by Cast Members who are willing to part with these special and emotionally charged pieces of Disneyana.

Special Event Pins are given out for attending exclusive engagements, tours, and activities at Disney. You could say that these pins are the most valuable pins to have because to get them you have to purchase the event ticket which usually comes with a high price tag. How do you collect these pins without paying $75.00 - $250.00 per person??? TRADE FOR IT!

Cast Member Recognition Pins are given to Cast Members who achieve milestone years of service and who are recognized for providing an exceptional guest experience. These pins can be specific to a division or group within Disney. For example Custodial and Laundry Services have some really cool pins that no one else can get.

Also, each division of WDC (the Walt Disney Companies) seems to have their own pin collections (WDI – Walt Disney Imagineering and WDBS – Walt Disney Burbank Studios would be two of these) and they can only be purchased or awarded to the Cast Members who work in that division and sometimes even at a specific location.

 Mᴏᴜꜱᴇ Pɪɴ Tʀᴀᴅɪɴɢ Tɪp!

Occasionally Pin Traders who represent the values of Disney Pin Trading get rewarded with one of these special pins that would normally be reserved for Cast Members. During a recent trip to the Magic Kingdom, my son was given a Top Dog Trader Pin for his patience, recognition of other traders, pin knowledge, and a firm handshake! It is now his favourite and most valued pin.

- **Exclusive Group Pins (D23, Club33)** are available only through exclusive membership clubs with Disney. D23 merchandise can only be purchased by D23 Club Members (available to all guests through a paid subscription) and include single pins and pin sets that are available to members only. Exclusive pins are also available at the annual D23 expo in Anahiem, CA.

Disney Club33 Pins are a little tougher to get as they are only sold within Club 33, the exclusive, members only restaurant in Disneyland. The last time I checked, there was a 14 year waiting list to join. If you see a Club33 pin, get it.

❤ **Disney Auction Pins** were sold online through disneyauctions.com until 2009 when it was amalgamated into thedisneystore.com. These pins pop up on the secondary market and can be identified by the "Gavel" imprint on the back and DISNEYAUCTIONS.COM on the back stamp.

♥ **Disney Soda Fountain Shop (DSF)** – Anyone for ice cream? The Disney Soda Fountain Shop is located on Hollywood Blvd in Hollywood, CA and I have to thank fellow Pin Trader, Erin, for introducing my family to DSF! On top of offering some of the most amazing ice cream creations in Southern California they also have an exclusive selection of pins. *All DSF pins are limited editions of 300* including their Pin Trader Delight Pin which only comes with the Pin Trader Delight Sundae. New DSF pins are released every month and these pins can be identified by the "Ice Cream Cone" imprint on the back.

♥ **Disney Resort Hotel Series** pins are released sporadically through Disney Resorts to guests of the resorts. These sets can contain 20 or more pins, so if you start to collect one of these sets, you need to bring your patience along. The pins will be marked "Disneyland (or WDW) Resort Hotel Series" on the back stamp.

♥ **The Disney Store (DS)** pins are sold (of course) through the Disney Store, either online or in the physical retail locations throughout the world. As well as offering their own pins, The Disney Store also retails D23 Member Pins and Disney Park Pins through the online store.

At peak times throughout the year, DS will offer Mystery Box Sets which will contain Limited Edition Pins with an edition size from 25 – 5000. Check out their sale section (previously known as Disney Outlet) for pin deals. The UK has a separate site, and offers a unique line of pins. Check out www.disneystore.co.uk to see the UK collection.

Mouse Pin Trading Tip!

Location Exclusives: Some locations, such as the Disney Store in Times Square, NY will offer exclusive pins that can make really neat additions to your collection. Look for the NYC Stamp on the back of the pin to make sure it's an exclusive NYC Pin. The New York Store recently changed from a World of Disney Store (on 5th Avenue) to a Disney Store (in Times Square) so you will find 2 types of pins from NYC, some that say "World of Disney" and some that just say "Disney Store NYC".

- **Disney Cruise Lines, Disney Adventures, AAA, Disney Vacation Club, Disney Visa, Disney Movie Club, and even Costco** all offer pins available for trading in the parks (as long as they say Disney) on the back and some of them are very cool.

Like we said earlier, there are over 90,000 pins in the Disney Pin Collection and it grows every day of the year so I am sure you will run into a few we haven't mentioned. If you find a pin you aren't sure of, you can check online at www.MousePinTrading.com for the pin database.

❤ **Vinylmation** – The hottest trend in Disney collectibles are Vinylmation 3D Rubber figures, so it was just a matter of time before they made their way to the Disney Pin World. The first run of Vinylmation pins were finished with cloisonné or hard enamel, but the latest editions mimic the rubber that the actual figures are made of. Disney has produced pins with rubber features on them for a long time, but the Vinylmation pins have so much rubber on them that Disney had to amend the Pin Trading Guidelines. The old rules state that the pins must be metal. The amended rules now state that a pin must have a metal back with the Disney Copyright to allow the Vinylmation pins to be traded, as the rubber front is fused to a metal back. This is so they will not be confused with the 100% rubber pins that have been produced in the past and are still not tradable in Disney Parks.

💗 **Pins To Avoid:** This section addresses the downside of Pin Trading. Like anything that is good and popular, there is always someone trying to take advantage. This applies to Disney Pins, so be aware. The golden rule applies: If it seems too good to be true, it probably is.

Scrappers are evil. When Disney Pins are produced, there are sometimes additional runs that get produced beyond the amount ordered by Disney. These are Black Market pins that are not authorized by Disney and may have subtle differences in color, size, detail or back stamp. Scrappers can be hard to spot, but as awareness of the fake pins increases so does the database of what to look out for. The majority of Scapper pins are in the Cast Lanyard Series so a good rule of thumb is that if the pin was released in Florida, but you see it in California on the day of release, it's probably a Scrapper. Quite frankly, I've been told so many contradictory ways of identifying Scrappers that I just use the same rule as I use for everything: If I like the pin and it looks legit, I trade for it. If it has rough edges, bubbles in the enamel or the color looks a bit off, I pass. You can do your part by not introducing these pins into the parks. How you ask? Only buy pins from reputable sellers and avoid buying from overseas where the pins are produced for Disney.

Pro Pins, Euro Pins & Sedesmas are pins that are produced for lower end retailers and the European market. They tend to be a lower quality and are not generally accepted as traders in Disney Parks. Sedesma Pins are produced in Spain while Pro Pins are made in Germany. These pins are not fakes like Scrappers, but they are avoided by pin traders.

Mouse Pin Trading Tip!

Remember why you're collecting Disney Pins: My daughter actually loves to collect the pins from Germany because they produce mini-pins in her favourite Disney Character - Tinkerbell. Although the pins may not have much value with other traders, they have value to her, because she likes them. As you build your pin collection, and interact with other Pin Traders, you will find many different opinions on what is valuable and what is not. The important thing is that it holds value for you.

So, now that you know just how many varieties of pins are out there, where do you start? What do you collect?

The good news is that there are over 90,000 pins out there. The bad news is that there are over 90,000 pins out there! That means that no matter what you decide to collect, there is plenty of inventory.

The best advice we ever got was to **collect what you like!** Don't worry about the value of the pin or what collection it's from. If you like it, collect it.

The only additional piece of advice we would add to that would be to figure out early on if you want to collect entire Hidden Mickey series or just the ones you like. The reason for this is because we switched channels and decided in our second year of trading that we were going to collect the entire HM series for that year and then had to deal with the fact that we had traded dozens of those pins away or simply not traded for them when they were available, so we had to go hunting for them again. Now when we find a HM pin, we trade for it, even though we might not have another pin that particular series.

The fun is in the finding of the pin and the story behind it. When you talk to Disney Guests and Cast Members about their pins, they don't rattle on about how much it's worth, but they will tell you every detail of how they found it and the story behind it.

Each pin tells a story. Maybe there is some history behind it's release or maybe it's a personal story about how you found it. It might be the animation history of the character featured on the pin or the development of a particular attraction that ties you to collecting those pins.

Whatever it is, take the time to talk to the Disney Cast Members and more experienced Pin Traders. It's amazing what you can learn by asking about a pin.

So, how do you get pins to start and avoid the $1,200 bill?!?

No worries, we've got you covered.

Pin Trading Essentials

Tools of the Trade:

To get started in trading Disney Pins, you need a few essential tools:

1. Something to put your pins on (or in)
2. A few extra pin backs
3. A big smile
4. A great attitude
5. Pins (obviously!)

Okay, so having pins is a no-brainer, but where can you buy them before you get to Disney? There are actually quite a few options open to you, but first, let's look at what else you need.

Something to put your pins on...

We've never seen anyone refuse to trade a pin with someone who kept their pins in a plastic bag, but there are better ways to manage your pin inventory! The most popular is an adult or child sized lanyard which hangs around your neck and holds your pins through the nylon mesh. These can be purchased through Disneystore.com or on EBay, and this is a great way to get your family into the excitement of trading as you can either choose or have them choose a lanyard with their favorite Disney character or theme.

We've seen people make their own lanyards out of strips of nylon ribbon and Velcro, but unless budget is a serious, concern, we recommend you invest the $8.95 in a proper Disney Pin Lanyard, to get you in the spirit.

You can also purchase Pin Starter Sets in a variety of character themes that include the lanyard. These sets usually retail between $24.95 and $44.95 depending on how many pins are included. The risk with these sets is that they came with really cool pins of your favorite character, so some folks (especially the younger ones!) have a hard time trading these pins away, or even trading back for them, so if you are going this route, try to find the sets that come with two of each pin, which gives you one to trade and one to keep.

8 Funky Mickey Pins you might want to keep...

1 Set to Keep ←

← 1 Set to Trade →

Once you've picked out your lanyard, you can personalize it even more with a Lanyard Medallion, which also helps keep your lanyard from bouncing around as you're running to get a picture with Tigger! Some of these medallions are Open Edition and some are a Limited Release or available only at Pin Trading events. Find one you like and attach it to the loop at the bottom of your lanyard.

If the thought of something hanging around your neck all day doesn't appeal to you, you might want to consider a Hip Lanyard or Pin Bag. The Hip Lanyard is a patch of nylon that hangs from your belt and the Disney Pin Bag is just what it sounds like... a shoulder bag that holds and displays your pins. They retail between $20.00 and $50.00, although you can sometimes get lucky on an EBay auction.

Pin bags are great when you are setting up shop in the park (at specified locations only) but they can get heavy and bulky when you are moving through the park and on and off the attractions. There are smaller versions available that work well and you can always put your trading pins on the strap itself if you like. Here are a few examples:

 ## Mouse Pin Trading Tip!

All Disney Pin Trading bags have 2 or 3 zippered pouches for holding extra pins, pin backs, pin lists and whatever else you can stuff in there plus velveteen pouches to display your pins. We were given a great tip from another Pin Trader (Thanks to Ron from Anaheim!) to put cardboard or foam board into the display pouches so that you don't have to deal with the pin backs when trading on a tabletop.

The board holds the pins securely and saves time (and pricked fingers) when moving the pins. Keep an eye out if you use the cardboard though, because the pins will eventually work loose. My personal preference is a double sheet of foam craft board.

Managing Your Pins, Once you get rolling and start running from Cast Member to Cast Member trading pins at every opportunity, you might find yourself forgetting what you have and what you don't have and when it comes to Hidden Mickey Pins, what you're collecting and what you aren't!

We have run into the unfortunate situation where we mistakenly trade away pins that we meant to keep, and nothing is worse than asking "Where's that pin that I've been looking for 6 months that I got today" and then vaguely remember trading it away because it was mixed in with your traders. It happened to us, so now we have a system... two systems actually.

Pin System 1: Keepers and Traders

Pick a side of your lanyard for keepers and another for traders. My daughter uses this system for her pins and she makes sure she knows which is which by putting an anchor pin on each side; Tinkerbell for keepers and a Puffle (those fuzzy things from Club Penguin) for Traders. Why Tink and a Puffle? Because Tink is her favorite and she doesn't have the same appreciation for the Puffles! That way, even in the frenzy of pin trading with multiple cast members, when she looks down at her lanyard, she knows exactly where to take the trader from and where to put the new find!

Simple but effective. But what happens when the Keeper Side gets full? Enter...

Pin System 2: The Bag Man

That would be me. Or maybe in your case, someone else in your group with the ability to be left holding the bag... of pins. I carry a smaller Pin Bag with two zipper pouches that hold only keepers for the entire group. This leaves the rest of the group to keep only traders on their lanyards. When they trade for a pin they want to keep, they give it to me and I put it in the back pouch.

If there is a pin they have traded up for (IE: Rack Pin for a Limited Edition or Completer Pin), but it's on the bubble, then I put it into the front pouch. Both pouches get emptied out at the end of the day, so we can decide as a group which pins to keep and which pins become more valuable traders.

Then we make note of what we still need to complete the series and restock the lanyards for the next day!

To keep your newly found pins secure, you might want to consider picking up a few extra Rubber Mickey Pin Backs, which secure your pins to your lanyard. Each pin you trade comes with an authorized pin back, but you will lose a back here and there, so it's a good idea to have back up. A package of Pin Backs can be purchased for under $3.00, but if you happen to lose one, simply ask a Cast Member if they have any extras.

Disney also sells Locking Pin Backs which are great if you have special pins that you want to display on your lanyard or pin bag. They come with a small Allan wrench to lock your pin in place and are very secure.

That covers all you need for the *physical* elements of Pin Trading, but we're not joking about the big smile and good attitude. When trading in the park, it can get pretty interesting when you meet someone who pushes through the line to get a pin they see on a Cast Member's lanyard. Pin Trading should be an enjoyable experience for everyone and when guests get impatient or rude, it brings everyone down.

Pin Trading Etiquette

We are going to copy the Pin Trading Etiquette Rules directly from the Disney Pin Trading site so that you have it for reference, but we would like to add a couple of points.

Point 1. When you see a Cast Member who is on task, be patient and polite. If they are doing something critical like serving another guest or setting up parade routes, please be respectful of their time. Make eye contact, let them know you are there and when they are done with their task, they will trade with you. We have even had Cast Members track us down to complete a trade after we thought they had ducked out.

If the Cast Member who you want to trade with is working a busy cash register in one of the retail locations, consider getting in line with the guests waiting to purchase their items. Once they know you want to trade, many Cast Members will take off their lanyards and let you browse while they look after other guests. It's a good idea to get a look at their pins from afar (without being creepy!) to see if there is anything you want a closer look at.

Hip lanyards have a tendency to flip over (or the Cast Member has turned it over on purpose) so use your discretion when asking to see their pins. We've never been refused, but there have been times when we definitely got the feeling we were interrupting... in pleasant way of course.

Point 2.　No matter who you are trading with, be respectful of them and their pins. This should go without saying, but some guests can get pretty enthusiastic when it comes to trading and they may not be familiar with the etiquette.

When we started trading, it took a while to get the rhythm and even longer for the kids to understand that they didn't have to trade with everyone they see. As you become more comfortable with pin trading, share your experience and knowledge with newer traders.

The idea behind pin trading is to meet people, so ask other Disney guests in line for attractions to see their pins. Worst case scenario is that you pass the time waiting to get on the attraction (especially good advice on Toy Story Mania!). We also carry a few extra pins around for "***Random Acts of Pinning***" where the kids give out pins to younger guests (with their parent's permission) who might not be as patient as we "more seasoned" Disney guests. It's amazing to see the reaction of the people around you and occasionally a nearby Cast Member has rewarded the kids for their generosity.

Okay, now that that's done, here's the Etiquette section from the Disney pin Trading Site:

Disney Pin Trading Etiquette

- Have Fun! Disney Pin Trading can be a great way to interact with and meet Cast Members and other Guests
- The main criteria to judge whether a pin is tradable or not is that it must be a metal pin that represents a Disney Event, Location, Character or Icon. Some pins from our Operating Participants are also tradable, but must represent the Operating Participant in a way that has a specific Disneyland® Resort or Walt Disney World® Resort affiliation.
- Pins should be in good, undamaged condition.
- Trade one pin at a time, hand to hand, with the backs attached.
- Guests may trade a maximum of two pins with each Cast Member.
- Guests may trade only one pin of the same style with a Cast Member.
- When trading with Cast Members, Guests should offer a pin that is not already displayed on the Cast Member's lanyard.
- Please refrain from touching another person's pins or lanyard. If you need a closer look, ask the person wearing the lanyard if they can bring it into clearer view for you.
- Disney name pins may not be traded with Cast Members.
- Monies or gifts may not be exchanged or used in trade for a pin.
- In addition to the 12 pins on Cast Lanyards, some Cast Members may wear a "Showcase" pin. These "Showcase" pins are for demonstrations to our guests and are not available for trade.

Now you've got everything you need... oh wait. What about pins?

Where to get your Trading Pins...

There are lots of places to get pins and some are more cost effective than others! You can wait until you are on your Disney vacation to get your pins, but I'm hoping that by now you have grasped the idea that that may be an expensive and stressful option (see Chapter 2) based on my family's experience. There is no reason for you to break the bank and you can have a good selection of trading pins before you leave for your Disney Dream vacation.

If you are going to wait until you arrive in the park to purchase your pins, make sure you purchase a few starter sets (the 7 pin or lanyard sets are a slightly better deal on a "cost per pin basis" and retail between $29.95 and $49.95) to get you rolling.

Here are a few other options for you:

EBay

If you are able to plan ahead, you can order your pins on line for a very reasonable cost per pin. Look for random pin lots that state that they have been traded in the Disney Parks and do not contain Scrappers, Propins or Sedesmas.

At least a month before you go (at this point, I always have an inventory of traders on hand) search EBay for "Disney Pin Collection". You will find pin lots of 10, 20, 25, and 50 and up to 200 and 300 that you can bid on and win at less than $1.00 per pin. Some creative auctions let you bid on the price per pin and then you select the amount you want to buy.

The reason I advise you shop at least 30 days prior to your trip is that you need the auction to end and allow enough time for shipping.

Some sellers will ship to your Disney resort, but I prefer to have them in hand before I leave!

Although you can find some decent "Buy It Now" pricing, you generally get a better deal through the auction. Remember, these pins are for trading, so you don't really care what pins are in the collection.

When purchasing pins online, there are a couple of points that I have found useful. If you are not familiar with purchasing on EBay, take some time to browse around and familiarize yourself with where the pertinent information is located.

Who Do You Buy from?

Personally, I don't buy from anyone with less than a 97.9% EBay score (preferably 100%) with a decent number of completed transactions (look for the EBay Preferred Seller Status) and decent feedback. Also, to avoid buying scrappers, I try to buy what looks like a collection instead of a "pin lot". You can pick up a decent selection of pins (sometimes with the bag) for around $1.00 per pin and you have a better chance of getting authentic Disney Pins. When you find a seller you like, save them to your Favorite Seller List so you can get notified when they have more pins for sale.

Choose a seller who agrees to ship within 1-3 days, with a tracking number if possible and estimate at least 5-10 days for transit and delivery.

Again, when you find someone you like, save them into your favorite sellers so you can go back to them for your next trip. If they ship to the Park resorts and you happen to run out of pins, they can be a handy resource who can hook you up with pins on short notice. (It happens!) Sellers from Florida and Southern California are obviously near the parks, so have access to newer pins, but I have great success with sellers from across the US and Canada.

Do You Buy From China or Europe?

It's up to you, but my preference is to shop within the US and Canada. In my experience, I have received a higher number of "Scrapper" pins from China and it's a bit suspicious when they send pins that aren't even in circulation yet! We already talked about "Scrappers", and how to spot them, but with great pin trading comes great responsibility (Disney owns Marvel Comics now, so it's okay to quote Uncle Ben from Spiderman) and it's a good thing to keep fake pins out of circulation as they devalue the real pins.

If you do choose to buy from Overseas, take note that it can take up to 45 days to receive your pins, so plan accordingly. Also make sure you know what the shipping costs are going to be before you bid.

What Pins Do You Buy?

Whatever fits within your budget! If you are intending on trading mainly with Cast Members then it doesn't matter how cool and funky your pins are. You are buying them to be traded, so you don't want to get emotionally attached to your pin inventory!

When buying on line, we try to bid on the biggest collections I can find within my budget, so I don't end up paying a lot of extra shipping charges. If bidding on multiple lots from the same seller, we make sure to ask for combined shipping so we don't get double charged.

Duplicates (in pin lot of 100 or more) are okay, especially if you are just starting out, as you will have some pins that you want to keep for your collection. Just like the pin lanyard sets, you now have one to keep and one to trade.

Shipping

Make sure you know what the shipping costs are before you bid and compare a few different sellers. As the pin market has become more competitive, many sellers are offering free shipping as an incentive. Always keep your "landed" or total cost in mind. Set a target price per pin (mine is 73 cents) including shipping, so you can stay on budget. Your goal should be to get as many pins as you can for your budget.

It's a good idea to know the approximate shipping costs so you don't get taken advantage of by sellers who are padding the margin on shipping. A Standard Rate USPS box can hold 100 pins and costs $4.95 (as of the time of this publication). Some sellers will add in a couple of bucks for their time, packaging and gas and I am fine with that as long as they tell you in the description and it's within budget.

SPECIAL NOTE FOR CANADIANS: Shipping to Canada from the US can be expensive, slow and limit the amount of sellers you can buy from. If you live within driving distance of the US border, there are numerous shipping houses that you can ship to for a small fee (My guy charges $2 per shipment) to avoid the issues. Some sellers don't like to ship to anything other than your PayPal address, so make sure they will ship to a third party address. If they won't ship, find a new seller; there are dozens of quality sellers who want your business.

PayPal

If you are new to EBay, you will need to set up a PayPal Account to pay for your transaction. Its EBay's preferred currency and you attach your account to a credit card or bank account. It takes minutes to set up and actually gives you insurance should you happen to have a dispute with the seller.

Remember why you're buying the pins – worth saying again!

FOR TRADING! You don't care if you have duplicates or how many Tinkerbell pins are in the lot, you're going to trade them away! There are always going to be a few keepers in any pin lot you buy, so bump your numbers by 10 or 20% to account for the AAAWWWWW LOOOOOKKKK AAAATTT THIIIIISSSSSS OOONNNEEEE!!!!! Factor.

It happens every time we get an order in… even with 2000+ pins in the collection!

Disney Outlet or Disney Character Outlet Stores.

I recommend to people who are visiting a Disney Park for the first time to stop by one of these stores before going to the park if they have time. These two chains are the authorized clearance locations for Disney Parks and you can find some huge discounts (up to 80% off) on all kinds of Disney merchandise including pins! The average price for pins here is between $5 and $7 but you can sometimes find even lower prices on pins they can't clear out or that are dated (IE: Bosses Day 2004!). We have found great pins for trading here, and we have also found just plain great pins. On our first trip to the Disney Character Outlet Store in Fullerton, CA, we found almost all of the Gold 50th Anniversary Character pins for $5 each that were tough to find on the secondary market.

You never know.

These stores come and go, but there are usually one or two around Orlando, FL and Anaheim, CA and they often put temporary locations in outlet malls throughout the US. We have personally found temporary Disney Outlet Stores (or partial Disney Outlet Stores) in Seattle, WA, Las Vegas, NV and Honolulu, HI, and actually completed Limited Edition Series from their sale inventory. It's a great way to find higher value pins below market value.

There is a link to these store locations on www.mousepintrading.com due to the changing locations of these stores.

The Disneystore.com

Disney used to run an online outlet store, but has since consolidated their online retail into one site. Click on the bottom of the page for SALE items which, of course, includes a decent selection of pins.

These pins are not usually better priced than in the Parks (in fact many of them are the same as they offer Park Merchandise, which can be handy if you get home and realize that you just can't do without that pin you saw in the Emporium or need to buy just one more Mystery Set), but they do go on sale from as low as $4.95 and, if you time it right, the seasonal boxed sets can be a great deal.

Make sure you pay attention to the shipping costs, as they can be expensive on smaller orders, and often run free shipping promotions with a minimum order.

Other Opportunities

If you live in California or Florida you will often find Disney Pins for sale on Craig's List and other online community services (Kijiji for one), but the majority of these listings are  Collectors who are looking to sell higher value collections.

For the local Disneyana Fan who doesn't mind getting up early and hitting the streets, you can find some pretty cool pins at garage sales and flea markets. I've met some Pin Traders in Disneyland who have found entire Vintage pin collections in garage sale give away boxes, but you better get there early and not rely too heavily on filling your trader quota the Saturday morning before you get to the park!

Personally, seeing as we don't live close to a Disney Park (my wife doesn't consider 23 hours of straight driving close), I keep track of which of my friends have been to Disney recently and when I see them, I ask "Did you collect any pins when you were there?" I know it's not rocket science, but it's amazing how many of them have pins they don't want and will offer to give them away! By the way, I generally trade a few smaller pins for a cool duplicate pin that I have on hand, so that I'm not taking advantage of them.

When we are in the park, we will also keep an eye out for pins that our friends collect and bring them back for them so they will return the favour when they go back.

Who do you know with a drawer full of Vintage pins they don't want?

In Disney Parks

Okay, so you bought the book, but didn't get around to following our advice. No worries, you can get your pins in the park. You will pay a lot more, but you can get your pins in the park.

Here's the deal. Get the most you can for your dollar.

When you're looking at pin sets, do the math on what it costs per pin versus the retail cost of the set. Last time I checked the best deal was the 7 pin set for $29.95 or $4.27 per pin.

When you are buying pins, I recommend purchasing in an actual Pin Store instead of the other 50 or so shops that have a pin display. The reason for this is that the pin stores will have the Gift with Purchase Collections and the other stores may not.

Check out what the amount is (usually around $30) and ask the Cast Member if you can get more than one Mystery (GWP) pin with a larger purchase or if you need to break it up into smaller purchases. Then work out the values so you can get the most Disney bang for your buck.

It's always better to group your purchases, but if you can't resist the urge to pop into the first store you see and buy pins, make sure you save your receipts. If you ask nicely, the Cast Member in the Pin Shop will usually let you add them up and then mark the receipt.

We have a complete and updated guide to the Official Pin Trading Store locations for each Disney Park at www.mousepintrading.com, so check it out before you leave.

Okay, so let's run a quick inventory:

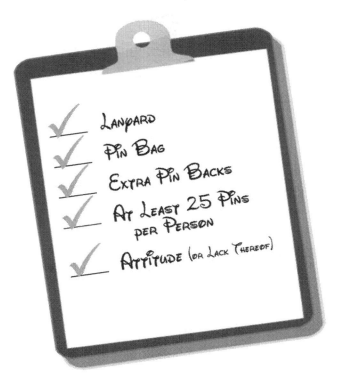

Checklist:
- ✓ Lanyard
- ✓ Pin Bag
- ✓ Extra Pin Backs
- ✓ At Least 25 Pins per Person
- ✓ Attitude (or Lack Thereof)

Alright, give everyone a High Five, take a deep breath, and let's go trade some pins!

Everyone's pin backs on tight? We are going to go through this point by point with the...

❤ **Do not leave any pins at home.** Bring the whole lot with you. Why? Because remember those pins that everyone fell in love with when you opened the package... well, you are about to enter a world where that experience is going to repeat itself every 20 feet or so... and Pin Traders are fickle creatures! What was an untradeable pin before you left home, can suddenly become fair game when you see a Cast Member with a cool pin of your favorite character or the one pin you need to complete a pin series. You can always take it back home with you.

❤ **If you are flying, put your pins in your carry on** as they can add pounds to your luggage. It's also kind of funny (as long as you have time) when the TSA agent asks you to show them your pins... slowly... so that they can have a look. Also if your pin bag is on the plane with you, you can kill some time going through your pins and checklists while you are in the air and maybe even trade a few pins on the plane. We usually end up giving away a few pins on the plane to families who are visiting Disney for the first time. Little do they know that the pin we gave them probably started them on a life of obsessive pin trading! Maybe next time, we should give them a copy of the book instead... and a pin.

💗 **Take your pins with you anytime you are doing** *anything* **Disney related**  (IE: Disney Soda Fountain or Downtown Disney) as you never know who will be trading pins. We got burned once at the Disney Soda Fountain Shop in Hollywood and it will never happen again. It was our last evening in LA and the Cast Member working the fountain had 3 pins we needed to complete our series. The good news was that the Soda Fountain has a store attached to it that sells discount pins so we only spent $15.00 on additional pins to trade!

Lesson learned – BRING YOUR PINS!

💗 **Be polite**. Although Disney Cast Members are open to trading (see Tip #2), they still have a job to do in the  park. If you see someone who you want to trade with, but they are in the middle of something or with another guest, be patient. Once they see you, they will generally acknowledge you and trade with you once they are done. If you are in a store and the Cast Member is at a busy cash register, you may want to get in line and wait with the people purchasing. If you ask to see a Cast Members pins and they have nothing you want to trade for, you are not obligated to trade, but again, be polite and thank them for their time. A little courtesy will go a long way with Disney.

- **Any Cast Member wearing a black lanyard must trade with you.** The only stipulations are that you can only trade up to a maximum of two pins per person and that the pin you are trading is not already on their lanyard. As long as they are wearing a Disney Cast Member Tag and a pin lanyard, you are good to go. A lot of Cast Members have moved to a Hip Pouch for trading, so you need to keep an eye out as they are harder to spot than regular lanyards.

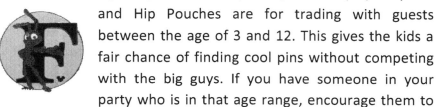

- **Child Only Lanyards.** Green (WDW) or Teal (DL) Lanyards and Hip Pouches are for trading with guests between the age of 3 and 12. This gives the kids a fair chance of finding cool pins without competing with the big guys. If you have someone in your party who is in that age range, encourage them to trade, as the Cast Members with the Child Lanyards are trained to be especially nice to the younger traders and will encourage them to keep trading. This means that as a parent you need to back off and let the magic happen.

- **Keep an eye out for Managerial and Custodial Staff.** Unlike the folks in the stores, these Cast Members move around more and may have a better selection of Hidden Mickey pins. Anyone wearing a suit in a Disney Park is doing a walk-through from one of the divisions and is usually loaded with pins! This is especially true early in the morning and at the start of the afternoon and evening shifts. Cast Pin selection tends to get less exciting as the evening wears on, but the evening shift Cast Members may have just the pin you're looking for. We've found some great pins after dark and the stroller traffic is tucked away for the night.

 In every park there are a few key places where Cast Members enter the park. If your main priority is trading for Hidden Mickey Pins, you can do quite well just hanging out and talking to Cast Members coming on-shift or off break who have just refreshed their lanyards! In Disneyland California, pay attention to the alley where the lockers are on Main Street, just behind the fruit stand. There's a great Ice Cream Shop down there too!

 If you happen to see the Mayor of Main Street in the Magic Kingdom, drop whatever you are doing and go trade. He wears multiple lanyards and is loaded with hard to find pins. Remember that the same rules apply so you can only trade 2 pins per person, however, if you are very courteous to the Mayor, you may receive a bonus pin.

 Start a conversation. All too often guests are in a hurry to trade and move on as there is so much to do and so little time to do it. However, we have found that when you take a little time to actually talk with the person you are trading with and take an interest in what they are doing or how long they have worked with Disney, good things happen. Most Cast Members have a bag of pins with them to restock their lanyards. When you take the time (1-2 minutes) to have a quick conversation, they may ask that magical question "Is there anything in particular you are looking for?" and pull out the extra inventory. We've had a lot of sets completed and received many perks (Fast Passes, Bonus Pins and even VIP Seating for Fireworks) just by being nice. And isn't getting to interact with people the real reason why you're trading pins in the first place?

♥ **Allow time to trade.** Nothing is more frustrating than having part of your group rushing to get on an attraction or meet a character and have someone stop every 20 feet to trade pins, and vice versa. The way we handle this is to have one of us take the tickets and go Fast Pass an attraction or get line for a character and meet back up with the pin traders. It really helps manage the time. NOTE: The person who goes on the errand should have pins with them just in case they see something worth trading for on the way!

♥ **Trade UP.** Not the movie... the value. Anytime we are trading in the park, we will always trade a pin that we brought with us for a higher value pin or a Hidden Mickey that we don't already have. Yes, this means you should trade for the funky looking High School Musical pin even if you don't like the movies! It's also a good idea to trade for any rare character pins you may come across as they may have value to someone who collects that character.

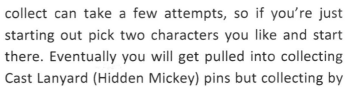

Collect in Sets or Characters. Figuring out what you want to collect can take a few attempts, so if you're just starting out pick two characters you like and start there. Eventually you will get pulled into collecting Cast Lanyard (Hidden Mickey) pins but collecting by character gives you a starting point. Also, most guests at Disney start out by buying starter sets in the park that retail between $22.95 and $49.95. This means that you can easily collect an entire set from Cast Members and save yourself a lot of money. Researching for this is simple, just pop into a store and look at the inventory. Make a note of how many pins are in the set and start hunting.

Other Trading Opportunities. Each Park in WDW has a pin book that is available to trade from. All you have to do is ask to see it at Guest Services or City Hall. Also, several stores and hotels will have a Pin Board (or shield, or post, or hat or Donald Duck and yes even a Pin Stroller!) that you can trade from. Sometimes they are out in the open but quite often you will need to ask to see them. There is a complete list of these locations in the member section at www.MousePinTrading.com which is continually being updated as new information comes available.

At certain times in Disneyland, just outside of the Westward Ho Trading Company Store in Frontierland, Cast Members will bring out pins bags for trading. This is a great opportunity to trade with a larger selection of pins and start trading with other guests who are in line to trade with the Cast Members. We've made some great trades and met some great people in these lines and quite often someone will track down a pin for you.

Professional Pin Traders are also in the parks (Disneyland and Epcot) and will have books of pins available for trade. We have met some who are phenomenal to deal with and some who, unfortunately seem to be there to take advantage of novice traders, so beware.

Mouse Pin Trading Tip!

A few rules to trade by with the "Big Guys" are: Trade Hidden Mickey for Hidden Mickey, Never purchase a pin from the store to trade for at their request and be respectful of their collections. It is quite likely to find pins that you have been looking for from their trading tables, but just make sure it's a good deal for both parties. Like any professional, they know what is valuable and what is not, and most are willing to share their knowledge and enthusiasm for pin trading, but like Jiminy says, *"Let your conscience be your guide..."*

Okay, that covers the basics of pin trading and other than walking you step by step down Main Street pointing out every Pin Trading opportunity, you should have all the information you need to get a head start over the uneducated Disney guest.

Just remember to have fun, talk to people and share your enthusiasm for the pins you find. We realize that some of the suggestions we make (*give* a pin away to a child...really?) don't lend to the hardcore, cut-throat world of collecting Disneyana, but that's the point.

We go to Disney Parks to get away from all that crud, so why would we promote a "GO get that pin at all costs" philosophy. It just makes people Grumpy... Here's what I mean.

By our third trip to Disneyland, we considered ourselves pretty savvy Pin Traders. We had completed numerous sets, had some pretty cool and valuable pins in the collection, and had even begun reselling some our pins online. In other words, we were ripe to be plucked.

At specific locations throughout Downtown Disney and Disneyland, there are tables set up for more advanced pin trading. We had noticed these tables and the people trading at them before, but had generally avoided them as we didn't feel "worthy" to trade with them and quite frankly they intimidated the kids.

 But on this trip we were ready. We had good pins. We had Limited Editions, Completers and Hidden Mickey Pins in volume! So as we were walking from the hotel to the park through Downtown Disney, my 11 year old daughter boldly approached a Pin Trader at the table outside of the Pin Traders Store and asked to see her pins. The lady looked her up and down and replied,

"Honey, you couldn't possibly have anything that I would be interested in", and closed her pin bag and turned her back.

Well, my daughter was devastated and my mouth was open to say something very Un-Disney-like when the Pin Trader at the next table said,

"Don't pay any attention to her, sweetie. She hasn't had her coffee yet. I would love to see your pins."

Crisis averted! This amazing lady understood she was dealing with a child attempting to step up to the next level of something she loved and that she had an opportunity to nurture instead of criticize. She patiently walked my daughter through her pin bag and told a few stories about her favorite pins and the people she traded them with.

At the end of it, we didn't have anything she wanted, but the experience was positive and we knew to keep an eye out for the pins she was looking for. As it turned out, we found two pins that she needed to complete the 2010 "Good Set" and competed a trade later in the day.

So what's the moral of the story?

Not everyone, even in "The Happiest Place on Earth" is going to have something you want to trade for, but that doesn't give you the right to be a (insert your choice of descriptive term here) and tear down their day. And that works both ways.

We've watched guests badger the heck out of Pin Traders and fondle their precious collections like they were at the flea market, and we've seen the Pin Traders smile and politely educate them on Pin Etiquette. On the flipside, there are, unfortunately, the rude traders like the lady my daughter encountered who are in it for the value of the pin, and that's fine. We know who we want to deal with and who we don't.

You also need to watch out for sharks... Pin Sharks (insert theme music from Jaws)...

Warning! Brutal honesty alert!

A Pin Shark is a trader who preys on new pin traders and takes advantage of their naivety (just wanted to get that word in somewhere!) to increase the value of their collection. They suck.

Here's the way a shark could potentially operate:

1. The Shark spots a potential victim – A Newbie with a shiny lanyard of newly purchased pins...
2. The Shark engages the victim in conversation and comments on their pins and how common they are...
3. The Shark falsely educates the Newbie on how valuable and rare the Shark's pins are compared to their pins, baiting the Newbie for an unequal trade.
4. The Shark lures the Newbie into trading a more rare or valuable pin (a lot of Newbies start out with $7 - $15 rack pins on their lanyards) for a common Hidden Mickey
5. The Shark may also lure the Newbie into trading multiple pins for one of their pins from the Shark's collection.

The best indicator for who is a Pin Shark is how the other Pin Traders react to them. If you see a lot of scowls or even avoidance, walk away. The Pin Traders we have met in the park tend to be a pretty close-knit group who have a lot of mutual respect for one another, so when they alienate someone, it's for good reason.

Also, be aware of "Guppies" who are children of Pin Sharks. They are pin savvy and will rook you out of your LE pins for a rack pin as fast as it takes to be amazed at their cuteness and pin trading intellect.

As a Pin Trader, you can figure out which type of Trader you want to be, but being courteous, polite and professional promotes trading, where the ones who are in it for the money deter new traders from continuing to trade and ultimately hurt their ability to trade with Disney guests.

Remember how I said that there were Pin Trading locations throughout Disneyland? Well, there used to be Pin Trading locations throughout Walt Disney World as well. Now the only place that Pin Traders can set up shop is in Epcot, outside the Pin Shop and traders are restricted to one pin bag and no chairs.

Why? Because guests complained about a few overly aggressive Pin Traders who were selling pins or asking guests to purchase pins to trade for. You have to respect the rules.

Every interaction we have with anyone in a Disney park is an opportunity for us to elevate or deflate them. When we are polite and take an interest in what they do, we leave that person feeling better about themselves, about us and about their Disney experience. That one or two minutes you take just might be the highlight of their trip!

Now, let's take your pin trading to the next level...

Advanced Pin Trading!

Really... *advanced* pin trading? Okay, so advanced might be a stretch. Pin Trading isn't, nor should it ever be an advanced science, but there are some things you might want to consider after you've got a few trades under your belt.

You might want to get the Pin Trading lingo down so you can sound like you know what you are talking about. The full Glossary of Terms is in the Resource Section at the end of the book.

Group Trading – Working the Park

Okay, you may have caught onto this already, but when you are more than a group of 1, you can work together to increase your effectiveness in the park. This also helps to get everything done on your "Disney To Do List" so you don't spend all day trading pins and suddenly realize you haven't done anything else!

This concept came from that first frantic trading trip to Disneyland. It didn't take long to figure out that the kids were trading over top of one another and competing for the same pins. It just wasn't healthy for fun in the park or a smart way trade, so we pooled our resources and started collecting as a group.

We still traded for our own favorite character pins, but when it came to collections, we worked to collect one complete series instead of four partial sets. Of course, if we saw a cool pin that one of our group would like, we traded for that too.

Trading as a group meant two things. We now had another fun family activity (and Disney Pin collection) and we could split up and work more than one area of the park. This also meant that two of us (or sometime just me) could go get Fast Passes while the rest of the group continued trading.

 Mouse Pin Trading Tip!

If you're the chosen one to go on the Fast Pass run, make sure you take your pins with you. The first time you run off without your pins is the time you will run into that pin you've been looking for forever. Unfortunately, I speak from experience.

Communication is critical when trading as a group so you don't duplicate your trades. Make sure you have a checklist! When we started trading Disney pins, we didn't have the Mouse Pin Mobile Checklist so we used a manual checklist (Thanks Pin Pics!) to keep track of our pin collections.

Now with the Mobile Checklist, we just upload our list and check them off as we locate them, but you can stick with the ream of paper lists if you like!

Setting Up Shop

When you think you're ready for it, grab a pin trading table and set up your pin bag full of traders. In California, there are Pin Trading tables outside the Pin Shop in Downtown Disney as well as inside Disneyland: in Frontierland outside of the Westward Ho! Trading Company Store (These are actually pin trading barrels) and in Tomorrowland outside of the Little Green Men Store. Disneyland will also run authorized pin trading days where traders will set up on the tables outside the Plaza.

Both Parks offer Pin Trading Nights (PTN's) where you can meet other Pin Traders and even get access to exclusive pins and a number of other perks. Check www.mousepinstrading.com or go to the official Disney Pin Site, www.disneypins.com for the latest schedule.

Remember the whole rant on being nice to guests and upholding the etiquette of Pin Trading?

With great pin trading power...

Working the Secondary Markets

There are numerous online pin trading communities (we like ours) and to find them just Google "Disney Pin Trading." For most of these sites the same rules apply and the sites are designed for trades only (no sales). It's a pretty cool way to expand your collection and never leave your couch.

If you leave the park and couldn't quite finish that Hidden Mickey Series or Mystery Set, you may be able to hunt it down on EBay. Some Pin Traders wont even speak the name of the online auction Giant (Like "You Know Who" in Harry Potter), but I have had a lot of success filling in sets when I know that I won't be back to the park for a while.

Finding a pin on EBay does not deliver even a smidgeon of the feeling you get when you find your "Holy Grail Pin" on a lanyard at a Disney Park, but there is some satisfaction in winning a cool pin at auction. As always, be on the lookout for fake pins.

The Final Trade of the Day...

Okay, I'm pretty sure that we've given you enough information to get a running start on your Disney Pin Trading Adventure! Just don't overcomplicate things. You will get excited, you will get slightly obsessed and you will spend some of your spare time online looking at pictures of cool Disney pins. It happens... and it's a great family experience.

Think about it. After you get back from most family vacations, you download the pictures, put away the souvenirs and that's the end of it until your parents or friends come over to see the slide show.

It's a memory. Which is nice, but...

When you come home with a lanyard full of Disney Pins, the first thing you do is pull out your *other* Disney Pins to put your collection together. Now you and your family are gathered around the kitchen table, pins glistening like pirate booty and talking about where each pin came from. By going through your pins, you relive each memory that is attached to that pin from every Disney vacation you've ever taken.

We have thousands of photos, hundreds of trinkets, framed memorabilia that we've picked up on vacation, and nothing comes close to the Disney Pins when it comes to having a really cool family moment. My kids will randomly pull out their pins and spend hours (usually when they should be doing their homework) going through the collection pin by pin.

How much is quality time between two teenagers worth in your house? ☺

Anyhoo… I hope you have found this guide useful. The following pages are full of Pin Trading Terms, Hidden Mickey Checklists and other useful resources that will keep you up to date.

We also have a ton of information and updates on the website www.mousepintrading.com and, of course, you have the mobile app to manage your collection when you're in the park!

Just one more thing…

Can we see your pins?

Seriously, go to the website and upload your collection in the member section.

Like the bouncy guy says… TTFN!

Resources

Disney Pin Street Lingo 101

- **AC – Artist Choice Pins.** Usually identified by a single paint brush and single pencil as the logo and reads ARTIST CHOICE on the Back Stamp.

- **AK – Animal Kingdom Park** located at Walt Disney World, FL. Also noted as DAK.

- **AOD – Art of Disney** Stores located throughout Disney Parks and Downtown Disney Districts. AOD stores often have guest artists who will sign and certify pins and artwork which make very cool additions to your collection.

- **AP – Annual Pass Holder** OR

- **AP – Artist Proof.** For every pin created there is a series of AP pins. The AP pins are usually the first 20-24 pins that are created during the artistic process. A copy of each pin developed is kept in the Disney Production Vault and the rest are released for sale. You can spot them by the small AP stamp on the back of the pin.

- **Back Stamp** – The information on the back of every Disney pin. Information may include the Disney Logo, Copyright info, Limited Edition Size, Where the pin was made (CHINA). Most recent pins include the Disney Pin Trading Logo and the year of release. The Back Stamp may also include what collection the pin belongs to and the size of the collection (IE: Hidden Mickey 2 of 5)

- **Build-A-Pin** – The Build-A-Pin program was introduced in 2002. Guests could personalize pins bases with character add-ons. After selecting their favorite base and add on, the pin was assembled with a special machine. The Build-A-Pin program was retired in Summer 2004.

- **Cloisonne** – Refers to that nice, shiny hard enamel finish that gives Disney Pins their high end look. The finish is hard baked using an open flame and then buffed to give a smooth hard finish.

- **CM** – Disney Cast Member

- **Continuing the Pin Trading Tradition Pin** – Also known as a **CTT** pin, these annual pins were created for guest recognition by cast members. Guests may be awarded a Continuing The Pin Trading Tradition pin for demonstrating positive Disney Pin Trading etiquette and promoting Disney Pin Trading.

- **D23** – The members club that offers exclusive merchandise including pins. Launched in 2010, there is an annual D23 Exposition in Anaheim, CA where you can meet artists, Disney actors and yes, trade Pins. Worth checking out at www.D23.com

- **DA** – Disney Auctions

- **Dangle-** A pin that has an additional feature suspended from the main body by a short length of chain.

- **DCA** – Disney's California Adventure Park in Anaheim, CA

- **DCL** – Disney Cruise Line

- **DEP** – Disney's Electrical Parade

- **DGS** – Disney Gallery Store

- **DHS** – Disney's Hollywood Studios

- **DL** – Disneyland Park in Anaheim, CA

- **DLP** – Disneyland Paris

- **DLR** – **Disneyland Resort** - referring to the whole area including hotels, parks and retail.

- **DLRP** – Disneyland Resort Paris

- **Domed Pins** – Domed Pins have a clear epoxy covering or plastic layer over the top of the pin.

- **DQ** – Disney Quest – The interactive arcade in Downtown Disney, Orlando, FL

- **DS** – Disney Store

- **DSF** – Disney Soda Fountain and Studio Store, Hollywood, CA – Just GO – Eat Ice Cream, and add some Limited Edition of 300 pins to your collection.

- **DTD – Downtown Disney District** – Located in both Orlando, FL and Anaheim, CA

- **DVC – Disney Vacation Club** – Make sure you stop by the booths located throughout the park, Downtown Disney and at various shopping centers throughout Orlando and Southern California (another reason to take pins wherever you go!) as they often get neglected and use pins as one way to speak with potential DVC Members.

- **Error Pins** – Not to be confused with Scrappers, these are actual Disney pins with a production error like a spelling mistake or a design error. Hey, it happens even at Disney!

- **Epcot** – is well, Epcot. We just felt bad because all the other WDW parks with long names got cool abbreviations. We just couldn't leave out the park that Figment calls home!

- **Exclusive** – A pin that is released at one location on one date. These pins are released to commemorate anniversaries and other momentous occasions and will only be available at the location that the pin in commemorating. For example, The Disneyana Shop in Disneyland.

- **Flipper** – Flipper pins have an additional painted area on the reverse side of the pin that can be flipped for an alternate view. It's like 2 pins in 1!

- **Flocked** – Just like a Christmas Tree, flocked means that the pin has a fuzzy surface.

- **FREE-D** – Free-D stands for Fastened Rubber Element on a pin for Extra Dimension. Pins that feature Free-D elements sometimes have discoloring issues, so look carefully before trading.

- **GWP** – Gift With Purchase (See Type of Pins section for details)

- **HG** – Holy Grail. The pin that you just gotta have!

- **HTF** – Hard To Find

- **JDS** – Japan Disney Store also known as TDS (Tokyo Disney Store) operated separately from the North American Disney Stores, but their pins are tradable in DL & WDW.

- **HHG** – The Hitchhiking Ghosts, are the most famous residents of the Haunted Mansion.

- **HM** – HM denotes either a Haunted Mansion or Hidden Mickey pin depending on the context.

- **Jumbo Pins** – Jumbo Pins are larger and often more intricately designed than a regular size pin, so the pins are more expensive that the regular size pins. These pins often come in elaborate packaging that adds to the look and presentation quality of the pin. NOTE: Check the Disney Character Outlet Stores for some deals on Jumbo Pins.

- **Lanyard** – The nylon strap that hangs around your neck to display your pins or Hip Lanyard that is a nylon pouch that hangs from your belt. Both styles come in a variety of colors and of course feature your favorite Disney Characters!

- **Lanyard Medal** – The medal serves 2 purposes: it weighs your lanyard down so it doesn't flop around as much and it looks really cool and personalizes your lanyard.

- **Light Up** – You guessed it, these pins have light up features that operate when you press or turn a button. Note, these take watch batteries, so a little maintenance is required.

- **M&P** – Mickey & Pal Shop in Japan. These stores operate under licence from Disney throughout Japan and the pins occasionally show up at WDW & DL.

- **Mickey's Mystery Pin Machine** – A bit of Disney Pin History! This debuted at Mouse Gear in Epcot at WDW in late 2007. The machines were a modified Gravity Hill arcade machine that dispensed a pin regardless of outcome. The pins were part of small collections consisting of five pins each. Although the pins originally cost $5 and were distributed randomly, remaining pins were sold as GWP pins and the Machines have now disappeared.

- **MGM** – Now known as Disney's Hollywood Studios Park in WDW as MGM Studios no longer exists!

- **MK** – Magic Kingdom (WDW)

- **MNSSHP – Mickey's Not So Scary Halloween Party**

- **Mint** – referring to a pin in perfect condition.

- **MSEP** – Main Street Electrical Parade (now known as Disney's Electrical Parade as DEP can at times been seen in both DCA and in MK at WDW. (just checking your acronym skills)

- **MVMCP** – Mickey's Very Merry Christmas Party

- **Mystery Pins** – also known as surprise pin that can be released at any time without advance notice.

- **Newbie** – Someone who is new to Pin Trading. We talked about this a lot in the trading section, but be nice and help educate the Newbies... we were all there once. Don't let them trade away their best pins just because they don't know any better.

- **Name Pins** - Name Pins are pins that have a name engraved on them, and may not be traded with cast members. Not to be confused with the Name Tag Series which are replicas of Disney Name Badges. If the pin says "Stitch" trade for it if it says "Irma" it shouldn't be there and leave it alone!

- **NBC** – Nightmare Before Christmas (fooled you didn't we?)

- **Pinbag** – Referring to an official or homemade bag designed to display and protect your pins.

- **P.I.N.S** – Stands for "Purchase It Now Store" which is what Disney Auctions was known as before they both went away in 2004. These pins pop up online all the time and are popular with collectors.

- **POH** – A Piece of History pin (POH) from the 2005 set is considered to be one of the rarest series in Disney Pin Trading. Each pin contains a minuscule piece of a prop from a WDW attraction. The first pin in the series, the 20,000 Leagues Under the Sea pin with a sliver of a porthole, has sold for over $275 on eBay. There have been numerous POH pin series (We have a chunk of an Autopia car from DL in our collection) and it's a cool way take home a piece of history and recycle at the same time! ☺

- **PT52 Pins** – are a series of 52 mystery pins that were sold in DL & WDW. The series features a wide variety of Disney Characters and no character repeats within the series. The only way to identify a PT52 pin is by the back stamp which says PT52. As an interesting twist Disney did not release list or pictures of the pins in the collection when the series released.

- **PTN** – Pin Trading Nights are monthly meetings of Disney Pin Traders at DLR, WDW, or Disneyland Paris resorts. The Pin Trading Team provides pin games and gives traders the opportunity to trade and socialize. Once in while an LE pin or Surprise Pin is released to commemorate the occasion.

- **Rack Pin, Open Edition or Core Pin.** – Yep, they are all one and the same. This simply means that the pins have no limit on manufacturing run and as long as they are selling, they will be available. Some of the pins that my kids "HAD TO HAVE" 7 years ago are still being sold today.

- **RSP** – This is straight off the Disney site. Make sure you check for updates as policy is subject to change! -The Random Selection Process is the method by which LE pins are distributed at the Pin Events. Each guest submits a form which has slots for the Limited Edition merchandise items offered. Each slot is filled in order based on pin availability. If 1000 forms were to be submitted and 50 forms had an LE 25 framed set in their first slot, the first 25 forms would be given the purchase, with the remaining 25 given the opportunity to purchase their second-slot pin. Typically, there are three rounds of the RSP process with the smaller editions being unavailable to purchase in subsequent round. RSP forms only allow a style of pin to appear once on each RSP form so that there is a better, fairer chance of each person getting one pin. (they should try this with concert tickets!)

- **SET, Series or Complete Set** – Are a collection of pins that have something in common and are generally offered as a numbered set (1of 10). The theme could be a character, movie, activity or the design format of the series (IE the T-Shirt series release in 2011)

- **Slider** – Those awesome little hamburgers... No wait. In Pin Trading, a Slider is a pin with a moving piece that slides back and forth.

- **Spinner** – A pin that has a section of the pin that spins 360 degrees and can be seen at all times... not to be confused with a Flipper which has 2 different sides and "Flips". Someone once told us that a flipper can spin, but a spinner cannot flip... and while we're at it, "Do you know why a Raven is like a Writing Desk?"

- **SPT or ST** – Super Pin Trader or Super Trader! You can spot these amazing people by the vest they wear covered in amazing pins! I mean you can see these guys from space... or at least across the park. An SPT will trade for any pin that they do not already have on their vest, but they are not Cast Members. Sometimes the pin you are trading must be in theme with the vest (Like all Stitch Pins), but this can be a fun and informative trading experience.

- **TDL** – Tokyo Disneyland

- **TDS** – The Disney Store

- **TTFN** – C'mon… you have to "figger" this one out for yourself!

- **VHTF** – Like Hard to Find, but with a Very at the beginning. A popular online descriptor.

- **WDC** – The Walt Disney Company

- **WDCC** – The Walt Disney Classic Collection. These are mainly Disney sculptures, but they do have a series of pins that go out to members.

- **WDI** – Walt Disney Imagineering. The folks who make all the magic happen behind the scenes, and yes, they have their own very, very cool pins.

- **WDW** – Walt Disney World – referring to the 4 main parks in Florida (Magic Kingdom, Hollywood Studios, Epcot and Animal Kingdom) plus the 2 Disney water parks (Typhoon Lagoon and Blizzard Beach) **WDW Resort** refers to the entire resort area including the on-site hotels, ESPN Sports Zone (or Wide World of Sports) and the Downtown Disney District. Each Disney Resort offers exclusive pins and may have a hotel series of lanyard pins at peak times during the year.

- **WOD** – World of Disney. The largest Disney stores on the planet located in Anaheim, CA and Orlando, FL. There was a WOD Store on 5th Ave in NYC, but it closed in 2009. There is now a Disney store in Time Square that offers pins unique to that location… and yes, they occasionally trade pins.

- **YOD** – **100 Years of Disney Pins** which were distributed through Disney Stores in 2001. The Set contains 99 core pins plus a pin for each state.

- **YOM** – **Years of Magic Pins** released for Walt's 100 Years of Magic Birthday Celebration in DL & WDW in 2001.

Hidden Mickey & Cast Lanyard Checklists...

Okay, so there are over 90,000 pins and we would love to provide a checklist for all of them, but we like the trees better as trees than as paper, so we have a large portion of those 90,000 pins on the website and you can create your own checklist with the mobile app! (Yeah trees!)

What you will find on the pages that follow is a checklist for each Hidden Mickey Series released from 2004 to 2011. Finding out what was included in each HM series took up a lot of time during our first two trips to Disneyland and we ended up getting wrong information and getting generally frustrated.

See, we didn't have this book! We think these are the definitive checklists and we've sorted them by collection, park, and the year they were released.

We hope you find it helpful!

So here's the deal with the Hidden Mickey Checklists...

When Disney started the Cast Lanyard Series (now known as the Hidden Mickey series), the pins were released and sometimes re-released in subsequent years, as the collection spanned more than one year. That's why you might see the same pin on a few different lists. On top of that, Disney would release some pins from WDW in DL and some pins from DL in WDW... Did that make you feel a bit Dopey?

Us too! In fact, figuring out what pin went with what year was one of the most confusing things for us when we started pin trading, as the date on the pin didn't always match the list. Most of this "Collection Confusion" happens in 2005-2007 (for a long time we referred to 2007 as the "Year of Hidden Mickey Pins" because we thought there were so many pins released!) because the pins sort of accumulate on the list. So, let's simplify...

If you have a pin, and it shows on different lists, it's the same pin. So check it off.

Just make sure that it is exactly the same pin. For example, Disney has released 4 different Monorail Sets between 2004 and 2011 and they are very similar.

Now that we've cleared that up... On to the lists!

NOTE: As you know, most of the Disney Pins are in color, and obviously this book is printed in black and white, so in some cases it may be hard for you to tell the colors of the pins on the checklists. That's why, when you go online to www.MousePinTrading.com and register your book, you will be able to printout full color versions of each of the checklists. Just follow the directions at the end of the book to get your checklists and other bonuses.

Also, some series have what are called "Completer Pins". On our checklists rather than listing them separately, we've put them with their series and highlighted them by putting a box around them, so you would know which ones are the "Completer Pins".

Disneyland® Resort
Pin Trading Lanyard Series II Pins (2004)

Winnie the Pooh - Seasons

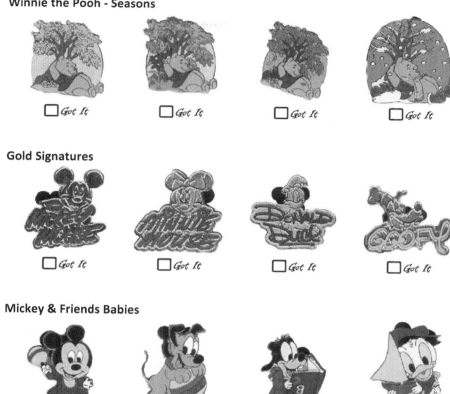

☐ Got It   ☐ Got It   ☐ Got It   ☐ Got It

Gold Signatures

☐ Got It   ☐ Got It   ☐ Got It   ☐ Got It

Mickey & Friends Babies

☐ Got It   ☐ Got It   ☐ Got It   ☐ Got It

Disneyland® Resort Pin Trading Lanyard Series II Pins (2004)

Western Hats

☐ Got It   ☐ Got It   ☐ Got It   ☐ Got It

Princes on Horseback

☐ Got It   ☐ Got It   ☐ Got It   ☐ Got It

Mickey & Minnie Exclamations

☐ Got It   ☐ Got It   ☐ Got It   ☐ Got It

Disneyland® Resort Cast Lanyard Collection 2.5 (2004)

Collection 1 – Unbirthday Series

☐ *Got It*   ☐ *Got It*   ☐ *Got It*   ☐ *Got It*

☐ *Got It*   ☐ *Got It*

Collection 2 – Kite Series

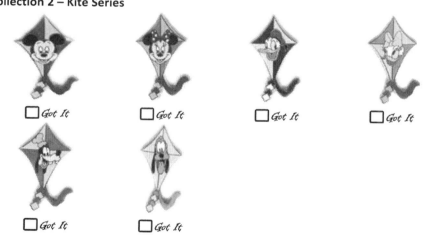

☐ *Got It*   ☐ *Got It*   ☐ *Got It*   ☐ *Got It*

☐ *Got It*   ☐ *Got It*

Disneyland® Resort Cast Lanyard Collection 2.5 (2004)

Collection 3 – Princess Star Collection

☐ *Got It*   ☐ *Got It*   ☐ *Got It*   ☐ *Got It*

☐ *Got It*   ☐ *Got It*

Disneyland® Resort Cast Lanyard Collection III (2005)

Collection 1 – Safari Series

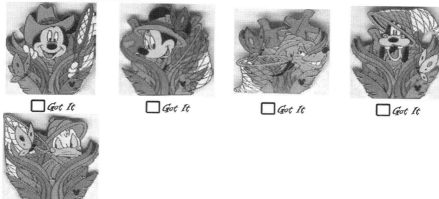

☐ Got It ☐ Got It ☐ Got It ☐ Got It

☐ Got It

Collection 2 – Nemo Pet Shop Bags

☐ Got It ☐ Got It ☐ Got It ☐ Got It

☐ Got It ☐ Got It ☐ Got It

Disneyland® Resort Cast Lanyard Collection III (2005)

Collection 3 – Surfboard Series

☐ Got It

☐ Got It

☐ Got It

☐ Got It

☐ Got It

☐ Got It

☐ Got It

Collection 4 – Fab 5 Sports

☐ Got It

☐ Got It

☐ Got It

☐ Got It

☐ Got It

Collection 5 – Mickey & Minnie Pin Trading

☐ Got It

☐ Got It

☐ Got It

☐ Got It

Disneyland® Resort Cast Lanyard Collection III (2005)

Collection 6 – Winnie the Pooh Dream Job Series

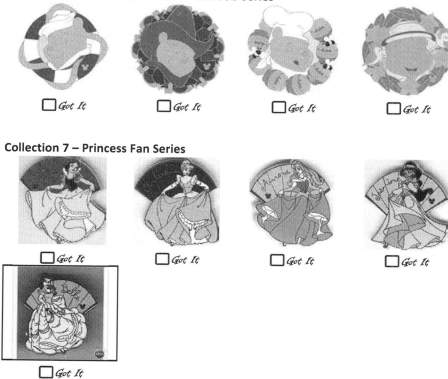

☐ Got It   ☐ Got It   ☐ Got It   ☐ Got It

Collection 7 – Princess Fan Series

☐ Got It   ☐ Got It   ☐ Got It   ☐ Got It

☐ Got It

Collection 8 – Tinkerbell Morning to Night Series

☐ Got It   ☐ Got It   ☐ Got It   ☐ Got It

Disneyland® Resort Cast Lanyard Collection III (2005)

Collection 9 – Mickey Ticket Series

☐ *Got It*

☐ *Got It*

☐ *Got It*

☐ *Got It*

☐ *Got It*

Collection 10 – Hatbox Series

☐ *Got It*

☐ *Got It*

☐ *Got It*

☐ *Got It*

☐ *Got It*

☐ *Got It*

☐ *Got It*

Disneyland® Resort Cast Lanyard Collection III (2005)

Collection 11 – Superhero Series

☐ *Got It*   ☐ *Got It*   ☐ *Got It*   ☐ *Got It*

☐ *Got It*

Collection 12 – Winnie the Pooh Cloud 9 Series

☐ *Got It*   ☐ *Got It*   ☐ *Got It*   ☐ *Got It*

Disneyland® Resort Cast Lanyard Collection IV (2006)

Collection 1 – Diamond Series

☐ *Got It*	☐ *Got It*	☐ *Got It*	☐ *Got It*
☐ *Got It*	☐ *Got It*	☐ *Got It*	☐ *Got It*
☐ *Got It*	☐ *Got It*	☐ *Got It*	☐ *Got It*

Collection 2 – Alice in Wonderland Pocket Watch Series 1

☐ *Got It*	☐ *Got It*	☐ *Got It*	☐ *Got It*
☐ *Got It*	☐ *Got It*		

Disneyland® Resort Cast Lanyard Collection IV (2006)

Collection 3 – Neverland Flight Series

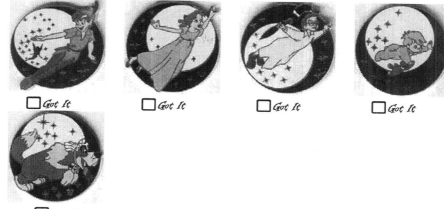

☐ *Got It* ☐ *Got It* ☐ *Got It* ☐ *Got It*

☐ *Got It*

Collection 4 – Beach Ball Series

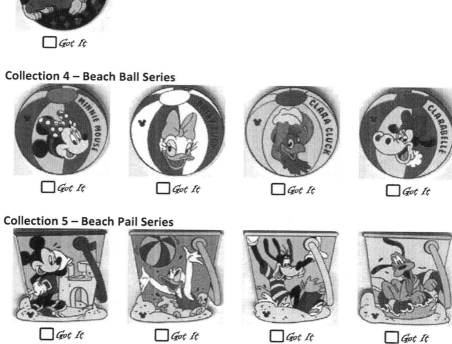

☐ *Got It* ☐ *Got It* ☐ *Got It* ☐ *Got It*

Collection 5 – Beach Pail Series

☐ *Got It* ☐ *Got It* ☐ *Got It* ☐ *Got It*

Disneyland® Resort Cast Lanyard Collection IV (2006)

Collection 6 – Tink & Pixie Friends Series

☐ *Got It*   ☐ *Got It*   ☐ *Got It*   ☐ *Got It*

☐ *Got It*   ☐ *Got It*   ☐ *Got It*

Collection 7 – Royal Couple Banner Series

☐ *Got It*   ☐ *Got It*   ☐ *Got It*   ☐ *Got It*

☐ *Got It*   ☐ *Got It*

Disneyland® Resort Cast Lanyard Collection IV (2006)

Collection 8 – Pirate Quote Series

☐ *Got It*   ☐ *Got It*   ☐ *Got It*   ☐ *Got It*

☐ *Got It*   ☐ *Got It*

Collection 9 – Muppets Circle Series

☐ *Got It*   ☐ *Got It*   ☐ *Got It*   ☐ *Got It*

☐ *Got It*   ☐ *Got It*

Disneyland® Resort Cast Lanyard Collection IV (2006)

Collection 10 – Villains Symbol Series

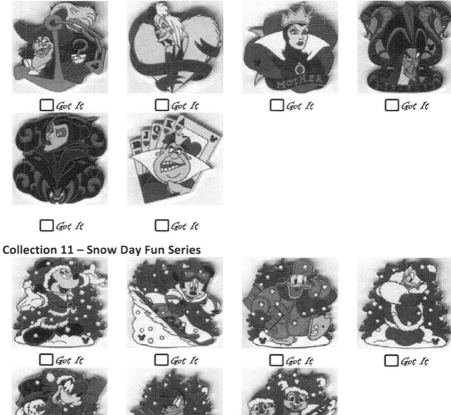

☐ *Got It*   ☐ *Got It*   ☐ *Got It*   ☐ *Got It*

☐ *Got It*   ☐ *Got It*

Collection 11 – Snow Day Fun Series

☐ *Got It*   ☐ *Got It*   ☐ *Got It*   ☐ *Got It*

☐ *Got It*   ☐ *Got It*   ☐ *Got It*

Collection 12 – Scrooge Mc Duck Pin Trading

☐ *Got It*   ☐ *Got It*   ☐ *Got It*   ☐ *Got It*

Disneyland® Resort 2007 Hidden Mickey Lanyard Pins

Collection 1 – Alice in Wonderland Pocket Watch Series 2

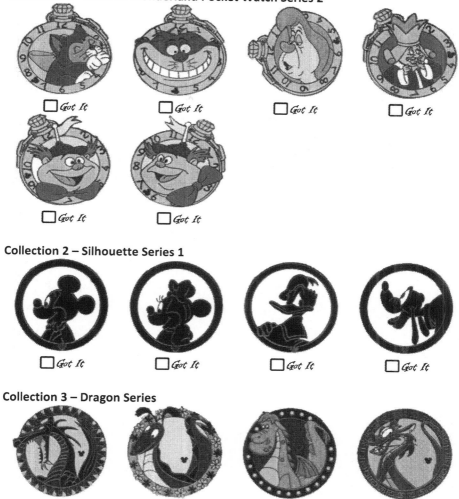

☐ Got It   ☐ Got It   ☐ Got It   ☐ Got It

☐ Got It   ☐ Got It

Collection 2 – Silhouette Series 1

☐ Got It   ☐ Got It   ☐ Got It   ☐ Got It

Collection 3 – Dragon Series

☐ Got It   ☐ Got It   ☐ Got It   ☐ Got It

Disneyland® Resort 2007 Hidden Mickey Lanyard Pins

Collection 4 – Fairies Flower Series

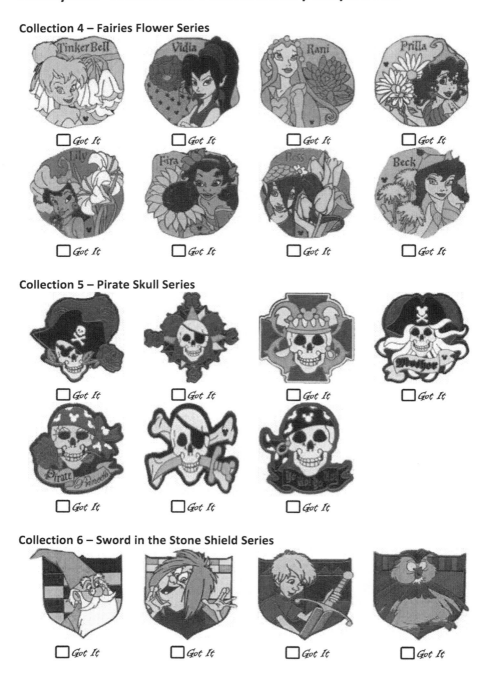

☐ *Got It*   ☐ *Got It*   ☐ *Got It*   ☐ *Got It*

☐ *Got It*   ☐ *Got It*   ☐ *Got It*   ☐ *Got It*

Collection 5 – Pirate Skull Series

☐ *Got It*   ☐ *Got It*   ☐ *Got It*   ☐ *Got It*

☐ *Got It*   ☐ *Got It*   ☐ *Got It*

Collection 6 – Sword in the Stone Shield Series

☐ *Got It*   ☐ *Got It*   ☐ *Got It*   ☐ *Got It*

Disneyland® Resort 2007 Hidden Mickey Lanyard Pins

Collection 7 – Princess Cartoon Bubble Series

☐ *Got It*   ☐ *Got It*   ☐ *Got It*   ☐ *Got It*

☐ *Got It*   ☐ *Got It*

Collection 8 – Chip 'N Dale Healthy Snack Series

☐ *Got It*   ☐ *Got It*   ☐ *Got It*   ☐ *Got It*

☐ *Got It*   ☐ *Got It*

Disneyland® Resort 2007 Hidden Mickey Lanyard Pins

Collection 9 – Villain Head Series

☐ *Got It*   ☐ *Got It*   ☐ *Got It*   ☐ *Got It*

☐ *Got It*   ☐ *Got It*

Collection 10 – Hitch Hiking Ghost Mirror

☐ *Got It*   ☐ *Got It*   ☐ *Got It*

Collection 11 – Donald's Halloween Series

☐ *Got It*   ☐ *Got It*   ☐ *Got It*   ☐ *Got It*

☐ *Got It*

Disneyland® Resort 2007 Hidden Mickey Lanyard Pins

Collection 12 – Mr. Toad's Wild Ride Cars Series

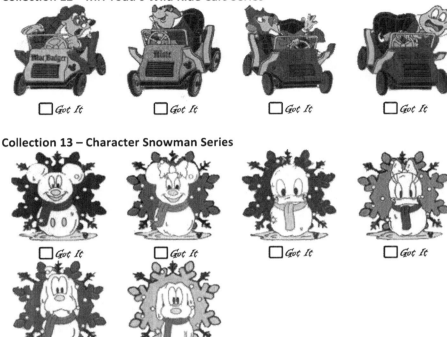

☐ *Got It*   ☐ *Got It*   ☐ *Got It*   ☐ *Got It*

Collection 13 – Character Snowman Series

☐ *Got It*   ☐ *Got It*   ☐ *Got It*   ☐ *Got It*

☐ *Got It*   ☐ *Got It*

Disneyland® Resort 2008 Hidden Mickey Lanyard Pins

Collection 1 – Character Silhouette Series 2

☐ Got It   ☐ Got It   ☐ Got It   ☐ Got It

☐ Got It   ☐ Got It

Collection 2 – Alice in Wonderland Chess Series

☐ Got It   ☐ Got It   ☐ Got It   ☐ Got It

☐ Got It   ☐ Got It

Disneyland® Resort 2008 Hidden Mickey Lanyard Pins

Collection 3 – Tink Teardrop Series

☐ *Got It*

☐ *Got It*

☐ *Got It*

☐ *Got It*

☐ *Got It*

☐ *Got It*

Collection 4 – Princess Gems Series

☐ *Got It*

☐ *Got It*

☐ *Got It*

☐ *Got It*

☐ *Got It*

☐ *Got It*

Disneyland® Resort 2008 Hidden Mickey Lanyard Pins

Collection 5 – Chip 'N Dale World Traveller Series

☐ *Got It*

☐ *Got It*

☐ *Got It*

☐ *Got It*

☐ *Got It*

☐ *Got It*

Collection 6 – Character Tiki Series

☐ *Got It*

☐ *Got It*

☐ *Got It*

☐ *Got It*

☐ *Got It*

☐ *Got It*

Disneyland® Resort 2008 Hidden Mickey Lanyard Pins

Collection 7 – Patriotic Star Series

☐ *Got It* ☐ *Got It* ☐ *Got It* ☐ *Got It*

☐ *Got It* ☐ *Got It*

Collection 8 – Military Heroes Series

☐ *Got It* ☐ *Got It* ☐ *Got It* ☐ *Got It*

☐ *Got It* ☐ *Got It*

Disneyland® Resort 2008 Hidden Mickey Lanyard Pins

Collection 9 – Back to School Series

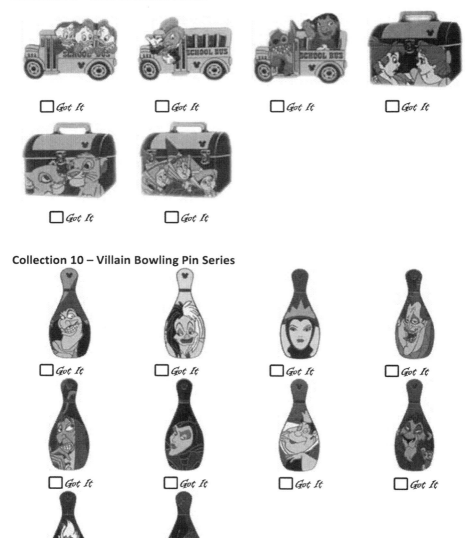

□ *Got It*   □ *Got It*   □ *Got It*   □ *Got It*

□ *Got It*   □ *Got It*

Collection 10 – Villain Bowling Pin Series

□ *Got It*   □ *Got It*   □ *Got It*   □ *Got It*

□ *Got It*   □ *Got It*   □ *Got It*   □ *Got It*

□ *Got It*   □ *Got It*

Disneyland® Resort 2008 Hidden Mickey Lanyard Pins

Collection 11 – Holiday Silhouette Series

☐ Got It   ☐ Got It   ☐ Got It   ☐ Got It

☐ Got It   ☐ Got It

Collection 12 – Holiday Crystal Series

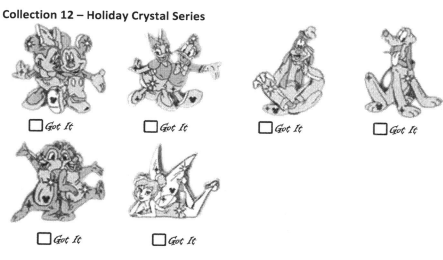

☐ Got It   ☐ Got It   ☐ Got It   ☐ Got It

☐ Got It   ☐ Got It

Disneyland® Resort 2009 Hidden Mickey Lanyard Pins

Collection 1 – Robin Hood Coin Series

☐ *Got It*   ☐ *Got It*   ☐ *Got It*   ☐ *Got It*

☐ *Got It*   ☐ *Got It*

Collection 2 – Small World Coin Series

☐ *Got It*   ☐ *Got It*   ☐ *Got It*   ☐ *Got It*

☐ *Got It*   ☐ *Got It*

Disneyland® Resort 2009 Hidden Mickey Lanyard Pins

Collection 3 – Neverland Chess Series

☐ *Got It*   ☐ *Got It*   ☐ *Got It*   ☐ *Got It*

☐ *Got It*   ☐ *Got It*

Collection 4 – Little Mermaid Shell Series

☐ *Got It*   ☐ *Got It*   ☐ *Got It*   ☐ *Got It*

☐ *Got It*   ☐ *Got It*

Disneyland® Resort 2009 Hidden Mickey Lanyard Pins

Collection 5 – 100 Acre Wood Silhouette Series

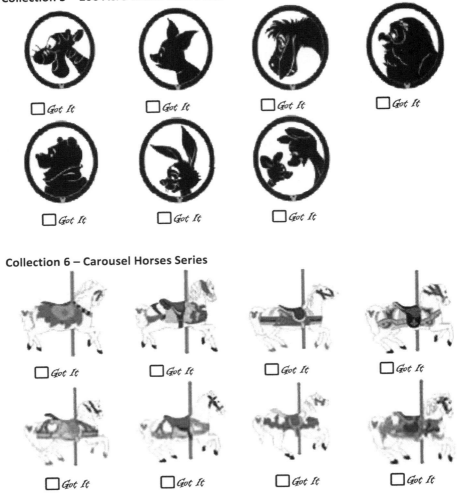

□ *Got It*   □ *Got It*   □ *Got It*   □ *Got It*

□ *Got It*   □ *Got It*   □ *Got It*

Collection 6 – Carousel Horses Series

□ *Got It*   □ *Got It*   □ *Got It*   □ *Got It*

□ *Got It*   □ *Got It*   □ *Got It*   □ *Got It*

Disneyland® Resort 2009 Hidden Mickey Lanyard Pins

Collection 7 – Patriotic Salute Star Series

☐ *Got It*   ☐ *Got It*   ☐ *Got It*   ☐ *Got It*

☐ *Got It*   ☐ *Got It*

Collection 8 – Haunted Mansion Tombstone Series

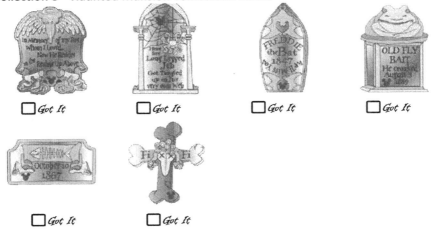

☐ *Got It*   ☐ *Got It*   ☐ *Got It*   ☐ *Got It*

☐ *Got It*   ☐ *Got It*

Disneyland® Resort 2009 Hidden Mickey Lanyard Pins

Collection 9 – Sepia Tone Snapshot Series

☐ *Got It*   ☐ *Got It*   ☐ *Got It*   ☐ *Got It*

☐ *Got It*   ☐ *Got It*

Collection 10 – Villains and Pets Series

☐ *Got It*   ☐ *Got It*   ☐ *Got It*   ☐ *Got It*

☐ *Got It*   ☐ *Got It*   ☐ *Got It*

Disneyland® Resort 2009 Hidden Mickey Lanyard Pins

Collection 11 – Princess Teacup Series

☐ *Got It*   ☐ *Got It*   ☐ *Got It*   ☐ *Got It*

☐ *Got It*   ☐ *Got It*

Collection 12 – Seven Dwarves Jack in the Box Series

☐ *Got It*   ☐ *Got It*   ☐ *Got It*   ☐ *Got It*

☐ *Got It*   ☐ *Got It*   ☐ *Got It*

Disneyland® Resort 2010 Hidden Mickey Lanyard Pins

Series 1 – Silly Symphony Series

☐ *Got It* ☐ *Got It* ☐ *Got It* ☐ *Got It*

☐ *Got It* ☐ *Got It* ☐ *Got It*

Series 2 – Black Cauldron Series

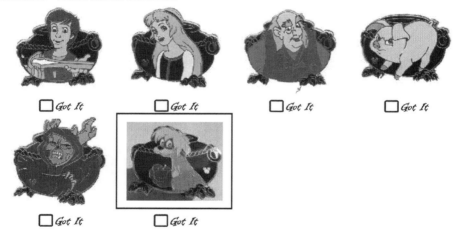

☐ *Got It* ☐ *Got It* ☐ *Got It* ☐ *Got It*

☐ *Got It* ☐ *Got It*

Disneyland® Resort 2010 Hidden Mickey Lanyard Pins

Series 3 – Character Holiday Ornament Series

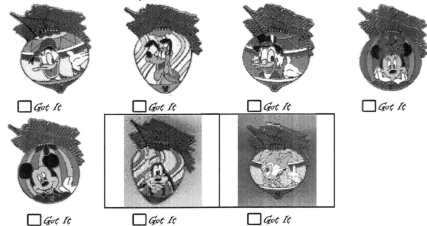

☐ *Got It*   ☐ *Got It*   ☐ *Got It*   ☐ *Got It*

☐ *Got It*   ☐ *Got It*   ☐ *Got It*

Series 4 – Princess Hearts and Butterfly Series

☐ *Got It*   ☐ *Got It*   ☐ *Got It*   ☐ *Got It*

☐ *Got It*   ☐ *Got It*

Disneyland® Resort 2010 Hidden Mickey Lanyard Pins

Series 5 – Disneyland Banner Series

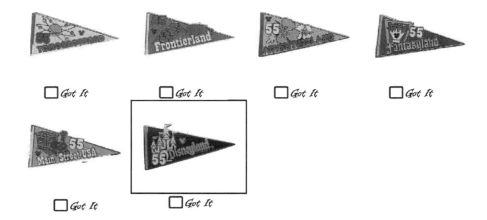

☐ *Got It*   ☐ *Got It*   ☐ *Got It*   ☐ *Got It*

☐ *Got It*   ☐ *Got It*

Series 6 – Aristocats Circle Series

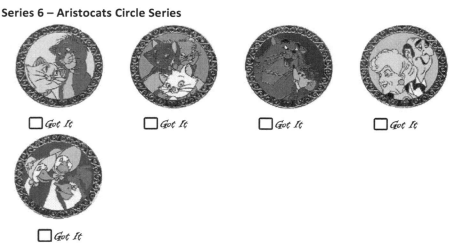

☐ *Got It*   ☐ *Got It*   ☐ *Got It*   ☐ *Got It*

☐ *Got It*

Disneyland® Resort 2010 Hidden Mickey Lanyard Pins

Series 7 – Country Bear Jamboree Series

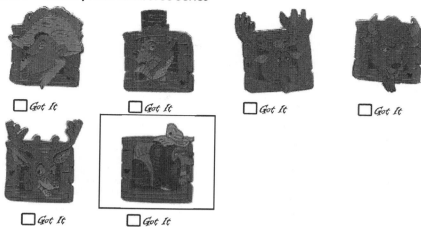

☐ *Got It*   ☐ *Got It*   ☐ *Got It*   ☐ *Got It*

☐ *Got It*   ☐ *Got It*

Series 8 – Villain Mirror Series

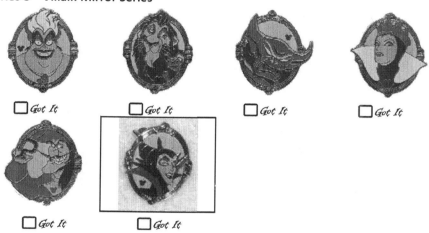

☐ *Got It*   ☐ *Got It*   ☐ *Got It*   ☐ *Got It*

☐ *Got It*   ☐ *Got It*

Disneyland® Resort 2010 Hidden Mickey Lanyard Pins

Series 9 – Alice in Wonderland 10th Anniversary Pin Series

☐ *Got It*   ☐ *Got It*   ☐ *Got It*   ☐ *Got It*

☐ *Got It*   ☐ *Got It*

Series 10 – Pop Bottle Series

☐ *Got It*   ☐ *Got It*   ☐ *Got It*   ☐ *Got It*

☐ *Got It*   ☐ *Got It*

Disneyland® Resort 2010 Hidden Mickey Lanyard Pins

Series 11 – NBC Candy Corn Series

☐ *Got It*   ☐ *Got It*   ☐ *Got It*   ☐ *Got It*

☐ *Got It*

Series 12 – Bed Knobs & Broomsticks Ribbon Series

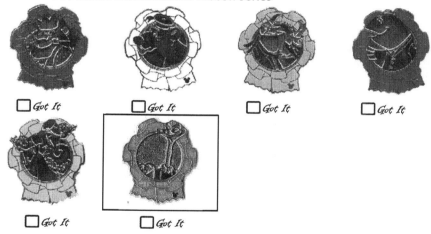

☐ *Got It*   ☐ *Got It*   ☐ *Got It*   ☐ *Got It*

☐ *Got It*   ☐ *Got It*

Disneyland® Resort 2011 Hidden Mickey Lanyard Pins

Mickey Mouse Around the World Series

☐ *Got It* ☐ *Got It* ☐ *Got It* ☐ *Got It*

☐ *Got It*

Casey Jr. Train Series

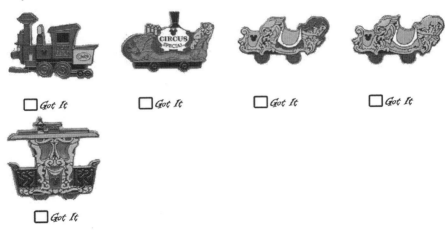

☐ *Got It* ☐ *Got It* ☐ *Got It* ☐ *Got It*

☐ *Got It*

Disneyland® Resort 2011 Hidden Mickey Lanyard Pins

DL Icon Series

☐ *Got It*

☐ *Got It*

☐ *Got It*

☐ *Got It*

☐ *Got It*

Fab 5 Portrait Series

☐ *Got It*

☐ *Got It*

☐ *Got It*

☐ *Got It*

☐ *Got It*

Disneyland® Resort 2011 Hidden Mickey Lanyard Pins

T-Shirt Series

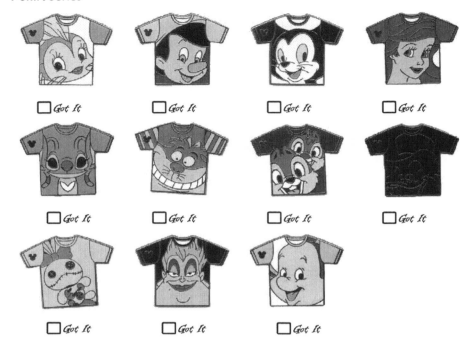

☐ *Got It*   ☐ *Got It*   ☐ *Got It*   ☐ *Got It*

☐ *Got It*   ☐ *Got It*   ☐ *Got It*   ☐ *Got It*

☐ *Got It*   ☐ *Got It*   ☐ *Got It*

Alice in Wonderland Comic Series

☐ *Got It*   ☐ *Got It*   ☐ *Got It*   ☐ *Got It*

☐ *Got It*

Disneyland® Resort 2011 Hidden Mickey Lanyard Pins

Monorail Series 4

Dark Blue/White	Light Blue	Red	Yellow
☐ *Got It*	☐ *Got It*	☐ *Got It*	☐ *Got It*

Dark Blue

☐ *Got It*

World of Color Fountain Series

☐ *Got It*   ☐ *Got It*   ☐ *Got It*   ☐ *Got It*

☐ *Got It*

Disneyland® Resort 2011 Hidden Mickey Lanyard Pins

Deebee Series

☐ *Got It*

☐ *Got It*

☐ *Got It*

☐ *Got It*

☐ *Got It*

Alphabet Series – Cut Out Letters

☐ *Got It*

☐ *Got It*

☐ *Got It*

☐ *Got It*

☐ *Got It*

☐ *Got It*

☐ *Got It*

☐ *Got It*

Disneyland® Resort 2011 Hidden Mickey Lanyard Pins

☐ Got It ☐ Got It ☐ Got It ☐ Got It

☐ Got It ☐ Got It ☐ Got It ☐ Got It

☐ Got It ☐ Got It ☐ Got It ☐ Got It

☐ Got It ☐ Got It ☐ Got It ☐ Got It

☐ Got It

Walt Disney World® Resort
Pin Trading Lanyard Series II (2004)

Series 1- Princess Hair Flip Series

☐ *Got It*   ☐ *Got It*   ☐ *Got It*   ☐ *Got It*

☐ *Got It*

Series 2 – Minnie Sunshine Series

☐ *Got It*   ☐ *Got It*   ☐ *Got It*   ☐ *Got It*

☐ *Got It*

Series 3 – 100 Acre Wood Baseball Series

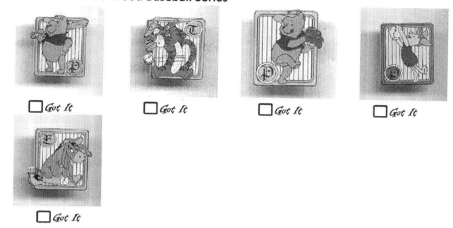

☐ *Got It* ☐ *Got It* ☐ *Got It* ☐ *Got It*

☐ *Got It*

Series 4 – Grey Tone Snapshot Series

☐ *Got It* ☐ *Got It* ☐ *Got It* ☐ *Got It*

☐ *Got It*

Series 5 – Mickey & Minnie Heart Series

☐ *Got It* ☐ *Got It* ☐ *Got It*

Walt Disney World® Resort Pin Trading Lanyard Series II (2004)

Series 6 – Character Initial Series

☐ *Got It*   ☐ *Got It*   ☐ *Got It*

Series 7 – Tink Flower Series

☐ *Got It*   ☐ *Got It*   ☐ *Got It*

Series 8 – Fishing Series

☐ *Got It*   ☐ *Got It*   ☐ *Got It*   ☐ *Got It*

Series 9 – Animal Sidekick Series

☐ *Got It*   ☐ *Got It*   ☐ *Got It*   ☐ *Got It*

Walt Disney World® Resort Pin Trading Lanyard Series II (2004)

Series 10 – Jungle Book Series

☐ *Got It* ☐ *Got It* ☐ *Got It* ☐ *Got It*

Series 11 – Dalmatian Bark Series

☐ *Got It* ☐ *Got It* ☐ *Got It*

Series 12 – Fairy Godmother Series

☐ *Got It* ☐ *Got It* ☐ *Got It* ☐ *Got It*

Series 13 – Pirate Coin Series

☐ *Got It* ☐ *Got It* ☐ *Got It* ☐ *Got It*

Walt Disney World® Resort Pin Trading Lanyard Series II (2004)

Series 14 – Scuba Series

☐ *Got It*   ☐ *Got It*   ☐ *Got It*   ☐ *Got It*

Series 15 – Lilo & Stitch Gold Leaf Series

☐ *Got It*   ☐ *Got It*   ☐ *Got It*   ☐ *Got It*

Series 16 – Villain Profile Series

☐ *Got It*   ☐ *Got It*   ☐ *Got It*   ☐ *Got It*

Walt Disney World® Resort Cast Lanyard Collection IV (2005/2006)

Series 1 – Princess Banner Series

☐ *Got It*   ☐ *Got It*   ☐ *Got It*   ☐ *Got It*

☐ *Got It*

Series 2 – Mickey Signature Series

Red   Yellow   White   Pink

☐ *Got It*   ☐ *Got It*   ☐ *Got It*   ☐ *Got It*

Black

☐ *Got It*

Walt Disney World® Resort Cast Lanyard Collection IV (2005/2006)

Series 3 – Muppets Name Series

☐ *Got It*　　☐ *Got It*　　☐ *Got It*　　☐ *Got It*

☐ *Got It*

Series 4 – Villain Cauldron On Series

☐ *Got It*　　☐ *Got It*　　☐ *Got It*　　☐ *Got It*

☐ *Got It*　　☐ *Got It*

Walt Disney World® Resort Cast Lanyard Collection IV (2005/2006)

Series 5 – Resort Sports Series

☐ *Got It*   ☐ *Got It*   ☐ *Got It*   ☐ *Got It*

☐ *Got It*

Series 6 – Tigger Sports Series

☐ *Got It*   ☐ *Got It*   ☐ *Got It*   ☐ *Got It*

Series 7 – Character in Tropical Shirt Series

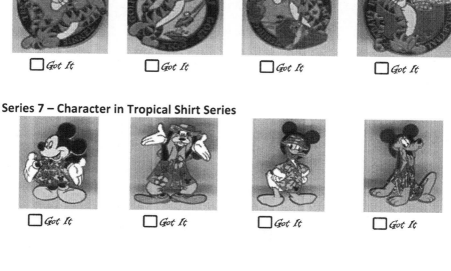

☐ *Got It*   ☐ *Got It*   ☐ *Got It*   ☐ *Got It*

Walt Disney World® Resort Cast Lanyard Collection IV (2005/2006)

Series 8 – Chip 'N Dale Dessert Series

☐ *Got It*   ☐ *Got It*   ☐ *Got It*   ☐ *Got It*

Series 9 – Character Parking Lot Series 1

☐ *Got It*   ☐ *Got It*   ☐ *Got It*   ☐ *Got It*

Series 10 – Figment Rainbow Series

☐ *Got It*   ☐ *Got It*   ☐ *Got It*   ☐ *Got It*

Series 11 – License Plate Series 1

☐ *Got It*   ☐ *Got It*   ☐ *Got It*   ☐ *Got It*

Walt Disney World® Resort Cast Lanyard Collection IV (2005/2006)

Series 12 – Fast Pass Series 1

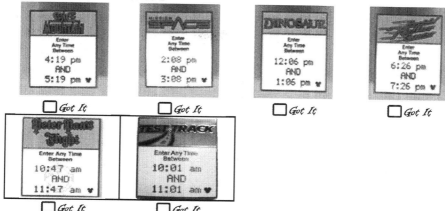

☐ *Got It* ☐ *Got It* ☐ *Got It* ☐ *Got It*

☐ *Got It* ☐ *Got It*

Series 13 – Coffee Mug Series

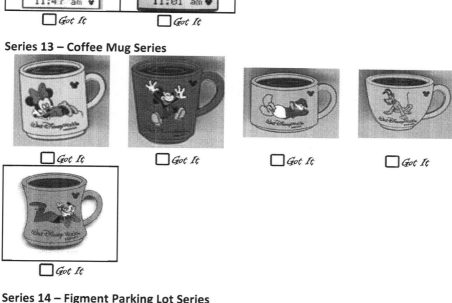

☐ *Got It* ☐ *Got It* ☐ *Got It* ☐ *Got It*

☐ *Got It*

Series 14 – Figment Parking Lot Series

☐ *Got It* ☐ *Got It* ☐ *Got It*

Walt Disney World® Resort Cast Lanyard Collection IV (2005/2006)

Series 15 – Monorail Series 1

Yellow   Grey   Purple   Orange

☐ Got It   ☐ Got It   ☐ Got It   ☐ Got It

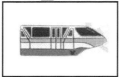

Pink

☐ Got It

Series 16 – Huey, Dewey, & Louie Series

☐ Got It   ☐ Got It   ☐ Got It

Series 17 – Stitch Space Series

☐ Got It   ☐ Got It   ☐ Got It

Walt Disney World® Resort Cast Lanyard Collection IV (2005/2006)

Series 18 – Tinkerbell Frame Series

☐ *Got It*   ☐ *Got It*   ☐ *Got It*   ☐ *Got It*

Series 19 – Pirate Icon Series

☐ *Got It*   ☐ *Got It*   ☐ *Got It*

Series 20 – Classic Mickey Head Series

Blue   Red   Yellow   Green

☐ *Got It*   ☐ *Got It*   ☐ *Got It*   ☐ *Got It*

Purple

☐ *Got It*

Walt Disney World® Resort Hidden Mickey Pins (2007)

Series 1 – Formal Series

☐ *Got It*   ☐ *Got It*   ☐ *Got It*   ☐ *Got It*

☐ *Got It*   ☐ *Got It*

Series 2 – Character Ticket Series

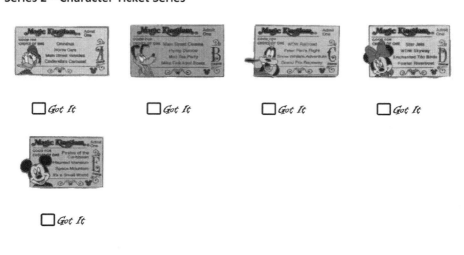

☐ *Got It*   ☐ *Got It*   ☐ *Got It*   ☐ *Got It*

☐ *Got It*

Walt Disney World® Resort Hidden Mickey Pins (2007)

Series 3 – Topiary Series

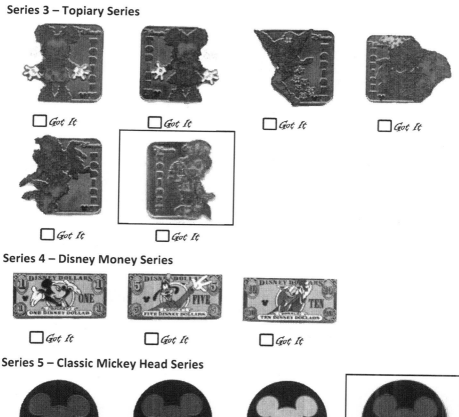

☐ *Got It*   ☐ *Got It*   ☐ *Got It*   ☐ *Got It*

☐ *Got It*   ☐ *Got It*

Series 4 – Disney Money Series

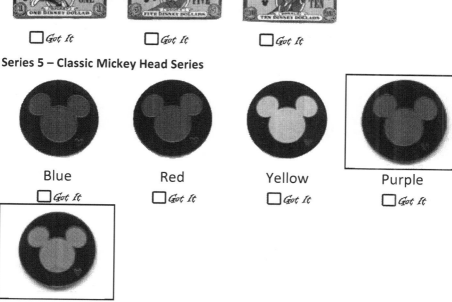

☐ *Got It*   ☐ *Got It*   ☐ *Got It*

Series 5 – Classic Mickey Head Series

Blue   Red   Yellow   Purple

☐ *Got It*   ☐ *Got It*   ☐ *Got It*   ☐ *Got It*

Green

☐ *Got It*

Walt Disney World® Resort Hidden Mickey Pins (2007)

Series 6 – License Plate Series 2

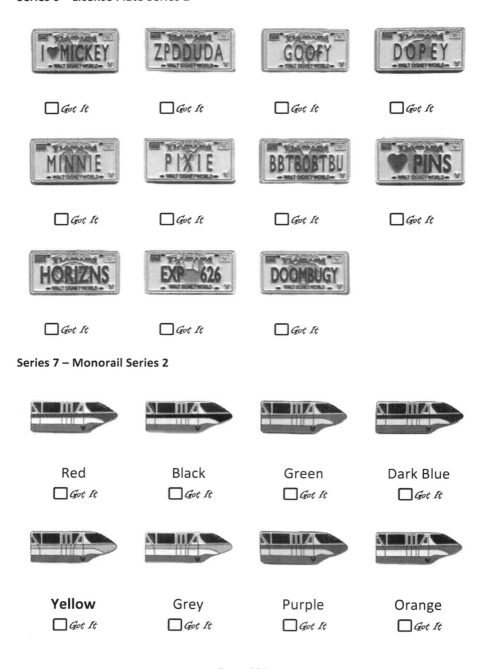

I ♥ MICKEY
☐ *Got It*

ZPDDUDA
☐ *Got It*

GOOFY
☐ *Got It*

DOPEY
☐ *Got It*

MINNIE
☐ *Got It*

PIXIE
☐ *Got It*

BBTBOBTBU
☐ *Got It*

♥ PINS
☐ *Got It*

HORIZNS
☐ *Got It*

EXP 626
☐ *Got It*

DOOMBUGY
☐ *Got It*

Series 7 – Monorail Series 2

Red
☐ *Got It*

Black
☐ *Got It*

Green
☐ *Got It*

Dark Blue
☐ *Got It*

Yellow
☐ *Got It*

Grey
☐ *Got It*

Purple
☐ *Got It*

Orange
☐ *Got It*

Walt Disney World® Resort Hidden Mickey Pins (2007)

Series 8 – Water Park Series

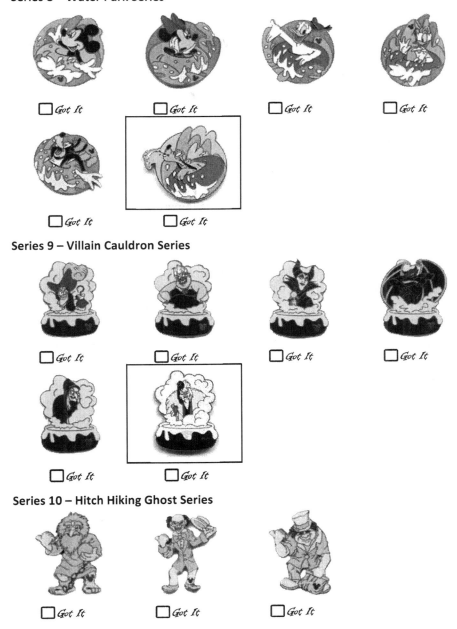

☐ *Got It*   ☐ *Got It*   ☐ *Got It*   ☐ *Got It*

☐ *Got It*   ☐ *Got It*

Series 9 – Villain Cauldron Series

☐ *Got It*   ☐ *Got It*   ☐ *Got It*   ☐ *Got It*

☐ *Got It*   ☐ *Got It*

Series 10 – Hitch Hiking Ghost Series

☐ *Got It*   ☐ *Got It*   ☐ *Got It*

Walt Disney World® Resort Hidden Mickey Pins (2007)

Series 11 – Fairy Godmother Series

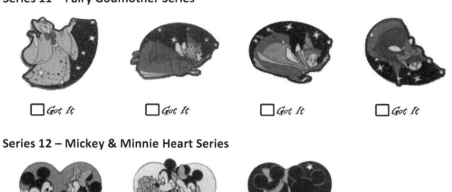

☐ *Got It* ☐ *Got It* ☐ *Got It* ☐ *Got It*

Series 12 – Mickey & Minnie Heart Series

☐ *Got It* ☐ *Got It* ☐ *Got It*

Series 13 – Pirate Icon Series

☐ *Got It* ☐ *Got It* ☐ *Got It*

Series 14 – Tink Frame Series

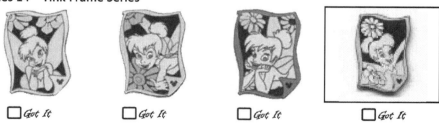

☐ *Got It* ☐ *Got It* ☐ *Got It* ☐ *Got It*

Series 15 – Scuba Series

☐ *Got It*   ☐ *Got It*   ☐ *Got It*   ☐ *Got It*

Series 16 – Pirate Coin Series

☐ *Got It*   ☐ *Got It*   ☐ *Got It*   ☐ *Got It*

Series 17 – Princess Banner Series

☐ *Got It*   ☐ *Got It*   ☐ *Got It*   ☐ *Got It*

☐ *Got It*

Walt Disney World® Resort Hidden Mickey Pins (2007)

Series 18 – Park Transportation Series

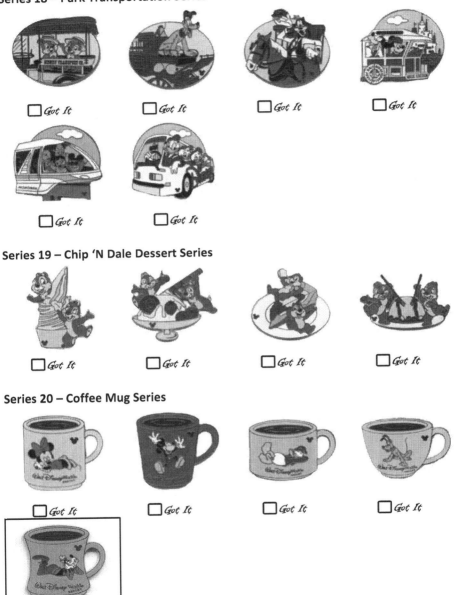

☐ *Got It* ☐ *Got It* ☐ *Got It* ☐ *Got It*

☐ *Got It* ☐ *Got It*

Series 19 – Chip 'N Dale Dessert Series

☐ *Got It* ☐ *Got It* ☐ *Got It* ☐ *Got It*

Series 20 – Coffee Mug Series

☐ *Got It* ☐ *Got It* ☐ *Got It* ☐ *Got It*

☐ *Got It*

Walt Disney World® Resort Cast Lanyard Collection III (2007)

Collection 1 – Princess Mirror Series

☐ *Got It*

☐ *Got It*

☐ *Got It*

☐ *Got It*

☐ *Got It*

Collection 2 – Mickey Dream Job Series

☐ *Got It*

☐ *Got It*

☐ *Got It*

☐ *Got It*

☐ *Got It*

Collection 3 – 100 Acre Wood Head & Arm Series

☐ *Got It*

☐ *Got It*

☐ *Got It*

☐ *Got It*

☐ *Got It*

Collection 4 – Wanted Poster Series

☐ *Got It*

☐ *Got It*

☐ *Got It*

☐ *Got It*

☐ *Got It*

Walt Disney World® Resort Cast Lanyard Collection III (2007)

Collection 5 – Character Ticket Series

☐ *Got It*

☐ *Got It*

☐ *Got It*

☐ *Got It*

☐ *Got It*

Collection 6 – Lightshow Series

☐ *Got It*

☐ *Got It*

☐ *Got It*

☐ *Got It*

Collection 7 – Park Transportation Series 1

☐ *Got It*

☐ *Got It*

☐ *Got It*

☐ *Got It*

Collection 8 – Park Transportation Series 2

☐ *Got It*

☐ *Got It*

☐ *Got It*

☐ *Got It*

Walt Disney World® Resort Cast Lanyard Collection III (2007)

Collection 9 – Character Parking Lot Series 2

☐ *Got It* ☐ *Got It* ☐ *Got It* ☐ *Got It*

Collection 10 – Figment Parking Lot Series 2

☐ *Got It* ☐ *Got It* ☐ *Got It* ☐ *Got It*

Collection 11 – Hollywood Studios Parking Lot Series

☐ *Got It* ☐ *Got It* ☐ *Got It* ☐ *Got It*

Collection 12 – Animal Kingdom Parking Lot Series

☐ *Got It* ☐ *Got It* ☐ *Got It* ☐ *Got It*

☐ *Got It*

Collection 13 – Adventureland Tiki Series

Collection 14 – Chip 'N Dale Junk Food Series

Collection 15 – Monorail Series 2

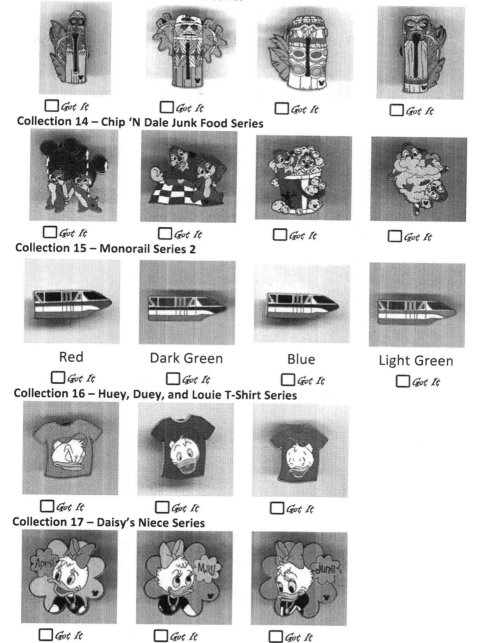

Red   Dark Green   Blue   Light Green

Collection 16 – Huey, Duey, and Louie T-Shirt Series

Collection 17 – Daisy's Niece Series

☐ Got It ☐ Got It ☐ Got It ☐ Got It

Walt Disney World® Resort Cast Lanyard Collection III (2007)

Collection 18 – HHG Series

☐ *Got It*

☐ *Got It*

☐ *Got It*

Collection 19 – Disney Money Series

☐ *Got It*

☐ *Got It*

☐ *Got It*

Collection 20 – 3 Caballeros Series

☐ *Got It*

☐ *Got It*

☐ *Got It*

Collection 21 – WDWR Icon Series

☐ *Got It*

☐ *Got It*

☐ *Got It*

☐ *Got It*

☐ *Got It*

☐ *Got It*

☐ *Got It*

Walt Disney World® Resort Hidden Mickey Pins (2008)

Series 1 - Duffy Series

☐ *Got It*   ☐ *Got It*   ☐ *Got It*   ☐ *Got It*

☐ *Got It*   ☐ *Got It*

Series 2 – Princess Eyes Series

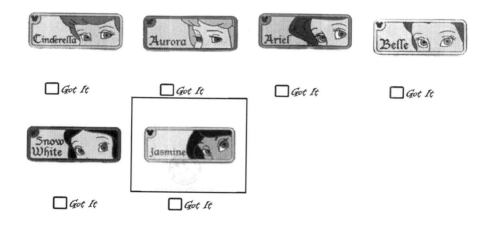

☐ *Got It*   ☐ *Got It*   ☐ *Got It*   ☐ *Got It*

☐ *Got It*   ☐ *Got It*

Walt Disney World® Resort Hidden Mickey Pins (2008)

Series 3 – Muppet Name Series 2

☐ *Got It*

☐ *Got It*

☐ *Got It*

☐ *Got It*

☐ *Got It*

Series 4 – Villain Crystal Ball Series

☐ *Got It*

☐ *Got It*

☐ *Got It*

☐ *Got It*

☐ *Got It*

Walt Disney World® Resort Hidden Mickey Pins (2008)

Series 5 – Donald WDW Land Series

☐ *Got It*   ☐ *Got It*   ☐ *Got It*   ☐ *Got It*

☐ *Got It*   ☐ *Got It*

Series 6 – Fast Pass Series 2

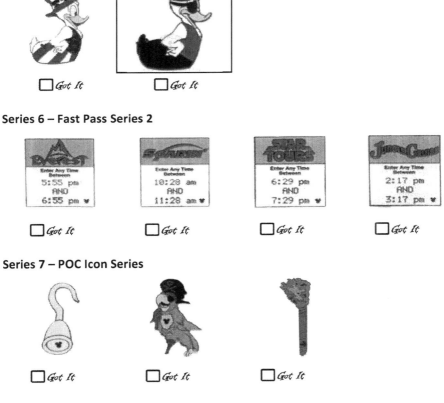

☐ *Got It*   ☐ *Got It*   ☐ *Got It*   ☐ *Got It*

Series 7 – POC Icon Series

☐ *Got It*   ☐ *Got It*   ☐ *Got It*

Walt Disney World® Resort Hidden Mickey Pins (2008)

Series 8 – Mickey Fruit Series

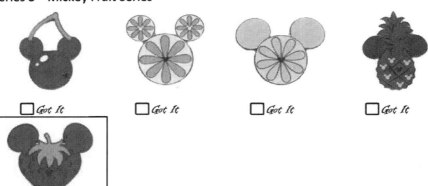

☐ *Got It* ☐ *Got It* ☐ *Got It* ☐ *Got It*

☐ *Got It*

Series 9 – Sidekick Series

☐ *Got It* ☐ *Got It* ☐ *Got It* ☐ *Got It*

Series 10 – Tiki in Mickey Ears Series

☐ *Got It* ☐ *Got It* ☐ *Got It*

Series 11 – Puffy Cat Series

☐ *Got It*

☐ *Got It*

☐ *Got It*

☐ *Got It*

☐ *Got It*

Series 12 – Figment Emotion Series 1

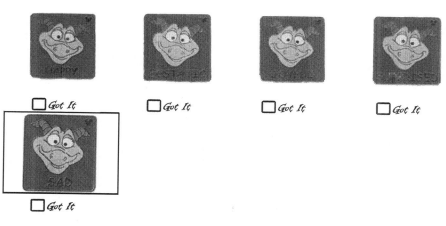

☐ *Got It*

☐ *Got It*

☐ *Got It*

☐ *Got It*

☐ *Got It*

Walt Disney World® Resort Hidden Mickey Pins (2008)

Series 13 – HM Icon Series

☐ Got It   ☐ Got It   ☐ Got It   ☐ Got It

☐ Got It

Series 14 – Monorail Series 3

Pink   Lime Green   Light Brown   Red

☐ Got It   ☐ Got It   ☐ Got It   ☐ Got It

Series 15 – Footprint Series

   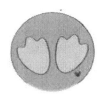

☐ Got It   ☐ Got It   ☐ Got It   ☐ Got It

Walt Disney World® Resort Hidden Mickey Pins (2008)

Series 16 – Pin Trading Logo Series

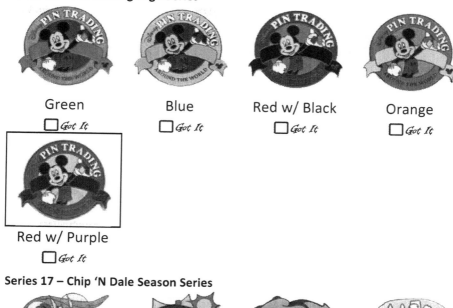

Green	Blue	Red w/ Black	Orange
☐ *Got It*	☐ *Got It*	☐ *Got It*	☐ *Got It*

Red w/ Purple
☐ *Got It*

Series 17 – Chip 'N Dale Season Series

☐ *Got It*   ☐ *Got It*   ☐ *Got It*   ☐ *Got It*

Series 18 – Tomorrowland Speedway Car Series

☐ *Got It*   ☐ *Got It*   ☐ *Got It*   ☐ *Got It*

☐ *Got It*

Walt Disney World® Resort Hidden Mickey Pins (2009)

Series 1 – Car Decal Series 1 & Car Decal Series 2

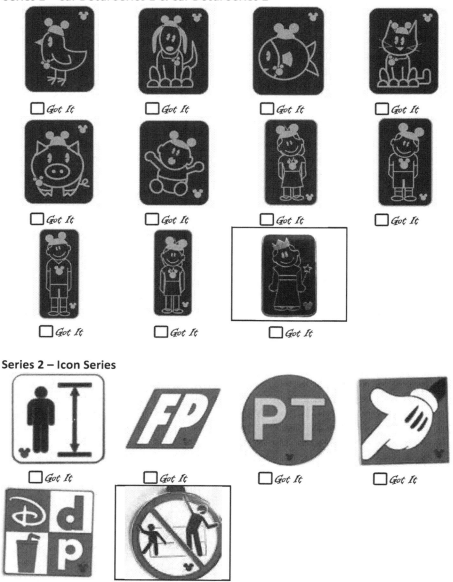

☐ *Got It* ☐ *Got It* ☐ *Got It* ☐ *Got It*

☐ *Got It* ☐ *Got It* ☐ *Got It* ☐ *Got It*

☐ *Got It* ☐ *Got It* ☐ *Got It*

Series 2 – Icon Series

☐ *Got It* ☐ *Got It* ☐ *Got It* ☐ *Got It*

☐ *Got It* ☐ *Got It*

Walt Disney World® Resort Hidden Mickey Pins (2009)

Series 3 – Chip 'N Dale Aloha Series

☐ *Got It* ☐ *Got It* ☐ *Got It* ☐ *Got It*

☐ *Got It*

Series 4 – Produce Mickey Head Series

☐ *Got It* ☐ *Got It* ☐ *Got It* ☐ *Got It*

☐ *Got It* ☐ *Got It*

Walt Disney World® Resort Hidden Mickey Pins (2009)

Series 5 – Figment Emotion Series 2

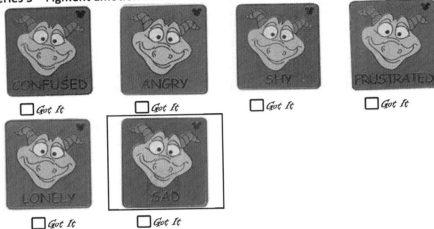

CONFUSED ☐ *Got It*

ANGRY ☐ *Got It*

SHY ☐ *Got It*

FRUSTRATED ☐ *Got It*

LONELY ☐ *Got It*

SAD ☐ *Got It*

Series 6 – Colorful Mickey Head Series

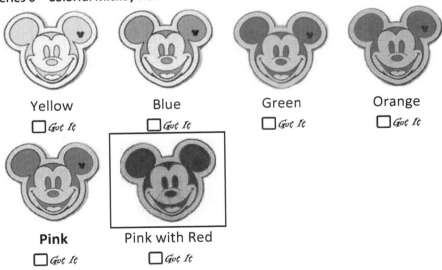

Yellow ☐ *Got It*

Blue ☐ *Got It*

Green ☐ *Got It*

Orange ☐ *Got It*

Pink ☐ *Got It*

Pink with Red ☐ *Got It*

Walt Disney World® Resort Hidden Mickey Pins (2009)

Series 7 – Park Icon Series

☐ *Got It*   ☐ *Got It*   ☐ *Got It*   ☐ *Got It*

☐ *Got It*   ☐ *Got It*

Series 8 – Character Sketch Series

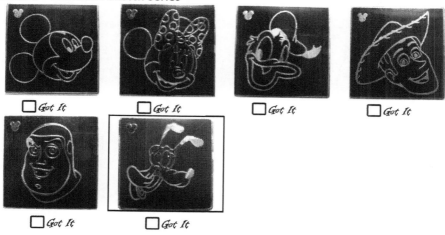

☐ *Got It*   ☐ *Got It*   ☐ *Got It*   ☐ *Got It*

☐ *Got It*   ☐ *Got It*

Walt Disney World® Resort Hidden Mickey Pins (2009)

Series 9 – Fast Pass Series 3

☐ *Got It*   ☐ *Got It*   ☐ *Got It*   ☐ *Got It*

Series 10 – Round Alphabet Series

☐ *Got It*   ☐ *Got It*   ☐ *Got It*   ☐ *Got It*

☐ *Got It*   ☐ *Got It*   ☐ *Got It*   ☐ *Got It*

Walt Disney World® Resort Hidden Mickey Pins (2009)

☐ Got It   ☐ Got It   ☐ Got It   ☐ Got It

☐ Got It   ☐ Got It   ☐ Got It   ☐ Got It

☐ Got It   ☐ Got It   ☐ Got It   ☐ Got It

☐ Got It   ☐ Got It   ☐ Got It   ☐ Got It

☐ Got It   ☐ Got It

Walt Disney World® Resort Hidden Mickey Pins (2010)

Series 1 – Main St. Character Series

☐ *Got It*   ☐ *Got It*   ☐ *Got It*   ☐ *Got It*

☐ *Got It*   ☐ *Got It*

Series 2 – Princess Heart and Butterfly Series

☐ *Got It*   ☐ *Got It*   ☐ *Got It*   ☐ *Got It*

☐ *Got It*   ☐ *Got It*

Walt Disney World® Resort Hidden Mickey Pins (2010)

Series 3 – Round Mickey Funky Series

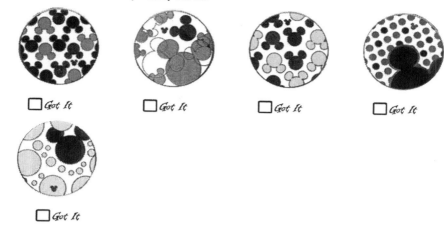

☐ *Got It*   ☐ *Got It*   ☐ *Got It*   ☐ *Got It*

☐ *Got It*

Series 4 – Figment Symbol Series

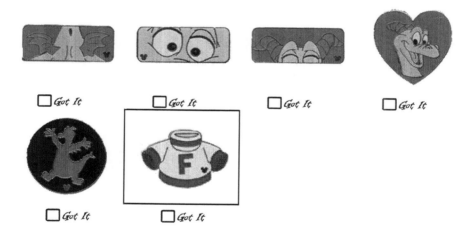

☐ *Got It*   ☐ *Got It*   ☐ *Got It*   ☐ *Got It*

☐ *Got It*   ☐ *Got It*

Walt Disney World® Resort Hidden Mickey Pins (2010)

Series 5 – Pin Trading Icon Series

☐ *Got It*   ☐ *Got It*   ☐ *Got It*   ☐ *Got It*

☐ *Got It*   ☐ *Got It*

Series 6 – Country Bear Jamboree

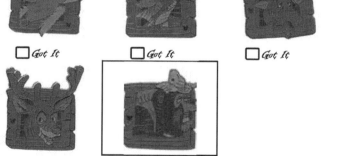

☐ *Got It*   ☐ *Got It*   ☐ *Got It*   ☐ *Got It*

☐ *Got It*   ☐ *Got It*

Walt Disney World® Resort Hidden Mickey Pins (2010)

Series 7 – WDW Banner Series

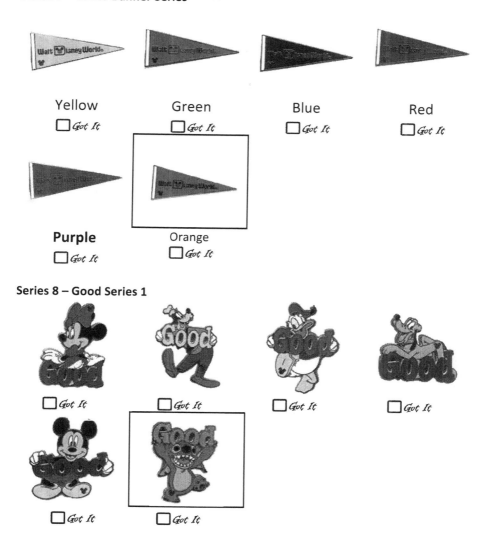

Yellow
☐ Got It

Green
☐ Got It

Blue
☐ Got It

Red
☐ Got It

Purple
☐ Got It

Orange
☐ Got It

Series 8 – Good Series 1

☐ Got It

☐ Got It

☐ Got It

☐ Got It

☐ Got It

☐ Got It

Walt Disney World® Resort Hidden Mickey Pins (2010)

Series 9 – Park Icon Series 2

☐ *Got It* ☐ *Got It* ☐ *Got It* ☐ *Got It*

☐ *Got It* ☐ *Got It* ☐ *Got It* ☐ *Got It*

☐ *Got It* ☐ *Got It* ☐ *Got It*

Series 10 – Colorful Mickey Series

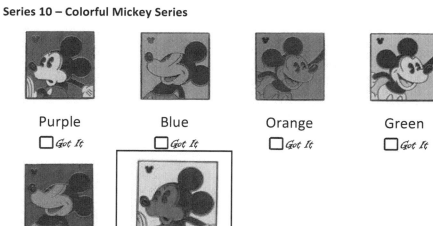

Purple Blue Orange Green

☐ *Got It* ☐ *Got It* ☐ *Got It* ☐ *Got It*

Red Yellow

☐ *Got It* ☐ *Got It*

Series 11 – Colorful Lanyard Series

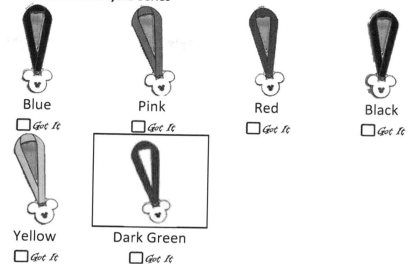

Blue	Pink	Red	Black
☐ *Got It*	☐ *Got It*	☐ *Got It*	☐ *Got It*

Yellow	Dark Green
☐ *Got It*	☐ *Got It*

Walt Disney World® Resort Hidden Mickey Pins (2011)

Series 1 – Good Series 2

☐ *Got It*   ☐ *Got It*   ☐ *Got It*   ☐ *Got It*

☐ *Got It*   ☐ *Got It*

Series 2 - Cute Yeti Series

☐ *Got It*   ☐ *Got It*   ☐ *Got It*   ☐ *Got It*

☐ *Got It*

Walt Disney World® Resort Hidden Mickey Pins (2011)

Series 3 - Orange Bird Series

☐ Got It ☐ Got It ☐ Got It ☐ Got It

☐ Got It

Series 4 – WDW DeeBee Series

☐ Got It ☐ Got It ☐ Got It ☐ Got It

☐ Got It

Walt Disney World® Resort Hidden Mickey Pins (2011)

Series 5 - Retro Icon Series

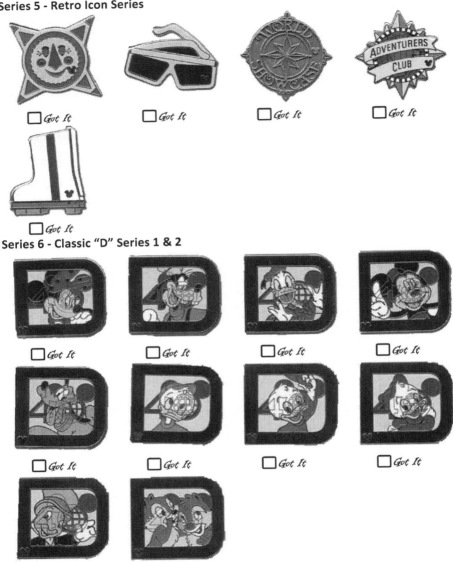

☐ *Got It*   ☐ *Got It*   ☐ *Got It*   ☐ *Got It*

☐ *Got It*

Series 6 - Classic "D" Series 1 & 2

☐ *Got It*   ☐ *Got It*   ☐ *Got It*   ☐ *Got It*

☐ *Got It*   ☐ *Got It*   ☐ *Got It*   ☐ *Got It*

☐ *Got It*   ☐ *Got It*

Walt Disney World® Resort Hidden Mickey Pins (2011)

Series 7 - Colorful Figment Series

Yellow   Pink   Purple   Blue

☐ Got It   ☐ Got It   ☐ Got It   ☐ Got It

Orange

☐ Got It

Series 8 – WDW T-Shirt Series

☐ Got It   ☐ Got It   ☐ Got It   ☐ Got It

☐ Got It   ☐ Got It   ☐ Got It   ☐ Got It

☐ Got It   ☐ Got It

Walt Disney World® Resort Hidden Mickey Pins (2011)

Series 9 - United Kingdom Icon Series

☐ *Got It*　　☐ *Got It*　　☐ *Got It*　　☐ *Got It*

☐ *Got It*

Series 10 - Princess Flower Series

☐ *Got It*　　☐ *Got It*　　☐ *Got It*　　☐ *Got It*

☐ *Got It*

Walt Disney World® Resort Hidden Mickey Pins (2011)

Series 11 – Silver Chaser Series

☐ *Got It*   ☐ *Got It*   ☐ *Got It*   ☐ *Got It*

☐ *Got It*   ☐ *Got It*   ☐ *Got It*   ☐ *Got It*

☐ *Got It*   ☐ *Got It*   ☐ *Got It*   ☐ *Got It*

☐ *Got It*   ☐ *Got It*   ☐ *Got It*   ☐ *Got It*

☐ *Got It*   ☐ *Got It*   ☐ *Got It*   ☐ *Got It*

Additional Resources
Places That Know Stuff About Disney Pins...

MousePinTrading.com – This is the official website for this book. If you haven't already visited the site and registered your copy of the book, please make sure to do that right now. Everyone who registers their copy of this book will receive our Mouse Pin Trading "PINsider" newsletter absolutely free. In the "PINsider", you'll find additional tricks and tips, special announcements including insider pin release information, and much, much more. You can also connect with us on Facebook at Facebook.com/MousePinTrading for the latest updates.

OfficialDisneyPins.com – This is the official site for Disney Pin Trading, and it's a great location to find the latest pin releases, Pin Trading Events, and links to all things Disney. Most of the info here will also be available on MousePinTrading.com, as we do our best to keep you up to date.

PinPics.com and DizPins.com – These two sites are related. PinPics has a large catalogue of Disney pin images and collections. Dizpins has a ton of general information on Disney Pin Trading. Be sure to check the date on the information, just to make sure it's been updated recently.

DizBoards.com – Another great resource for information provided by fellow Pin Traders, and actually has a great list of who to buy from (and not buy from) on eBay if you want to avoid buying scrappers. Check out the links for up to date blog posts.

MouseEars.com and MouseSavers.com – These sites provide general information, and are not related to Pin Trading, but ever since our very first trip to Disneyland, these are the two sites I check for deals and Disney info. After all, the more I save on hotels and food, the more pins I can buy, right?!?

Register Your Book...

We've mentioned this a few times throughout the book, and I know that there will be some of you who haven't done this yet, so here are the final instructions for registering your book.

Go to http://www.MousePinTrading.com and on the right side of the page, you'll see a banner that says "REGISTER MY BOOK". Once you click on that banner, you'll be taken to a page where you can register your copy of this book. You'll need to enter your name, email address, and if you want, your address and phone number. You'll also be able to select a username and password to access the member's only area of the website where you will be able to print out the color versions of the checklists.

Registered Members of MousePinTrading.com get:

- The "PINSider" Newsletter
- Access to Print Color Versions of the Different Checklists that are in the book and many more lists
- Updates about upcoming special events, including possibly some local pin trading events in cities around the globe
- Special access to all the latest updates to this book
- Preview Access to some of the upcoming Premium features of the website including:
    - An Interactive Pin Database
    - Upload Your Personal PINventory
    - Print Customized Checklists of Your Most Sought After Pins
    - Much, Much More...

Don't Miss Out, Register NOW, and we'll see you at the park...

My Pin Notes...

My Pin Notes...

My Pin Notes...

My Pin Notes...

My Pin Notes...